EDUCATOR EXTRAORDINARY

The Life and Achievement of Henry Morris

ACKNOWLEDGEMENTS

We are grateful to Cambridgeshire and Isle of Ely County Council and to Walter S. Morris for permission to reproduce 'The Village College', 1924, by Henry Morris.

We are grateful to *The Architectural Review* for permission to reproduce Plate 6 and to E. Maxwell Fry and *The Architects Journal* for permission to reproduce the plan on page 76.

EDUCATOR
EXTRAORDINARY

The Life
and Achievement
of Henry Morris
1889–1961

Harry Rée

LONGMAN

Longman Group Limited
London

*Associated companies, branches and
representatives throughout the world*

© Longman Group Ltd 1973

First published 1973
ISBN 0 582 36312 8

Printed in Great Britain by
Western Printing Services Ltd
Bristol

AUTHOR'S NOTE

At least a dozen friends of Henry Morris have, over the past ten years, been discussing and planning a book about him. Material was collected carefully by Mrs Dorothy Bimrose, his secretary for fifteen years; friends collaborated by writing recollections and sending her letters and papers. All this material has been made available to me, and without it I would not and could not have written the present book; all quotations made without source reference are taken from it. It is therefore a cooperative production and I have to thank countless collaborators. Almost all are mentioned in the text. One in particular should be mentioned here. If Charles Fenn had not let me have his letters, a very different and less lifelike hero would have emerged from these pages. I do not think I will be the only one to feel grateful to him.

H.A.R.

CONTENTS

Contents

HENRY MORRIS 1889–1961

Henry Morris is the begetter of the Community School. He invented and created the Village College. He introduced the New Architecture to school building, and put colour and original art into classrooms. He advocated the abolition of the 'insulated school' and promoted radical curriculum reform; he was the first to put forward a workable scheme for lifelong education and community control of schools. All this he did while Chief Education Officer of Cambridgeshire, from 1922 to 1954.

He was an outsider. His public life was colourful, so was his private life. He was oddly enchanting and often maddening. Very generous at times, at times he could be mean and even petty. Fiercely independent, but hating being alone. A homosexual who was repelled by the effeminate, and who believed firmly in the family. An ex-elementary schoolboy and convinced socialist whose style of life was aristocratic. He inspired undetachable loyalty but made, and kept, many implacable enemies.

Like a rocket he lit up the dark skies of the thirties. After the war he began to decline. By the end of his life he was burnt out. But he remains a force today, and not a diminishing one.

I THE MAN

Best begin at his home. In his house in Trinity Street, Cambridge, above what was then Farringdons ('the hairless art shop' he used to call it), Henry Morris received guests in a first-floor room of great elegance. A gilt-framed Georgian mirror between the symmetrical windows, a long Ivon Hitchens above the mantelpiece, mahogany bookshelves, a great sofa covered in yellow silk, delicate tables on the white carpet, and a jungle of books, papers, letters with vases of flowers between.

Arriving on a Saturday evening I'd be sent out with a scribbled cheque to King's College buttery for a bottle of sherry. Over drinks he'd talk about the building plans for his next projected scheme, about Gropius, about insensitive dons ('all piss and cinders'). Others would arrive from London – dinner table talk about pictures, love, salads, politics, architecture. Evening music on the inappropriate looking radiogram – Mozart opera with coffee from very light white Coalport cups – time to sleep – upstairs to the attic bedrooms, icy cold in spite of a tiny coal fire which glowed in the ancient little grate, creaking iron bedstead with a paper thin mattress. (About these beds one of his friends wrote: 'They were the type which used to be known as "emergency hospital", and were liable to collapse even under one occupant.') Sunday morning – the papers, two or three Cambridge friends arrive. Then, the Walk. Across the meadows to Cantaloupe Farm, to Haslingfield, or to Granchester or Madingley. Monologue from Henry on rural education, on colours, scorn for the self-indulgent and unrealistic British Communists, utter intolerance for British capitalists 'with faces like plates', anecdotes about 'filleted' parsons with their fluted voices, or women dons – 'their wombs are stuffed with algebra', quotations from Meredith, Wordsworth, Eliot, Shelley (he was a great quoter). Beer and sandwiches in the aimed-for pub. Those walks have been vividly recalled by many of his friends. Ian Phillips has written:

They showed Henry at his most characteristic and delightful. Swinging his ashplant walking-stick and carrying a battered rucksack on one shoulder, sometimes plodding through heavy rain, and accompanied or followed in two's or three's by talkative or enthralled friends. He would launch into some favourite topic, emphasising his words from time to time with wild swipes at imaginary *bêtes noires* . . . I remember a disquisition on architecture and gardens which took place in a pub. As we left, the concrete statue of a gnome caught Henry's eye, and with a suitable explosion about mass-produced non-art he raised his stick and neatly severed the object's head. He was as astonished as the owner at this only half intended result.

Jacquetta Hawkes gave this description:

We carried sandwiches in our pockets. I think Henry was always a little ashamed of the scene when we all opened our packets in the pub; it didn't at all please his high sense of elegance. He walked with long strides, but would stop suddenly, often turning right round, driving his stick into the ground when he wanted to denounce or to praise something. And he had a curiously fastidious way of negotiating gates or fences.

And a rather more reluctant walker, Norman Fisher (who was his assistant at Shire Hall and later became Chief Education Officer of Manchester), remembered, as a 'necessary qualification' for associating with Henry Morris, having 'to walk over many miles of mudstained countryside on Sunday mornings eating one's lunch in damp discomfort among the dreary bar parlours of Cambridgeshire, and in fine weather, plunging with well simulated enjoyment into cold river water and if necessary drying oneself on one's shirt'.

Back to tea at his house. Local friends and guests taking the London train would disperse. For those staying overnight there would be a quiet evening. A simple supper always with a green salad. For this, invariably, Henry would take a Georgian silver table spoon and mix in it, with a fork, the French dressing. First the salt and pepper, then a little vinegar, then the olive oil. The lettuce was then anointed. It was a regular and cheerful ceremony. After supper, more music, more talk, and early bed.

He was concerned more than most people with appearances, including his own. He wore his carefully chosen clothes with a convincing insouciance. He might look untidy but he was obviously aware of the colours and materials which suited his blue eyes and healthy complexion and his height. 'I have the nicest ties in Cambridge,' he once said. Very occasionally he wore an Irish tweed kilt – claiming that his right to it came through his mother's family. Once he had his tailor make for him a magnificent flannel suit of hunting pink. Sometimes he would put it on in the evenings but in the end he had it dyed black.

Jacquetta Hawkes has vividly recalled his presence:

When I first met Henry in the early forties he was still a very handsome man. If he himself had not been living behind it, one might say that his face was lacking in detail and peculiarity, too much like a girl's sketch of a handsome man. But then of course Henry *was* behind his face and made expressive use of it. In repose there was something troubled, even desolate, behind those preposterously bright blue eyes. When he talked his expression changed with the words and their moods – much more than is usual except in the heroes of not very good novels.

Addressing an audience Henry could look and speak like a prophet, with telling passion and authority. I have seen a large council of worldly and successful men so moved by his address on what our cities were like and what they might become, that for an hour or so they had faith that something could and must be done. In private conversation he was very different. Usually a humorous gleam came into his eyes and he spoke through a smile, a half mocking smile. Then when he had finished he would look up at one confidently sharing his recognition of the follies of the world, and at the same time the possible absurdities of his own denunciations. His face characteristically showed his blend of self appreciation and self deprecation. A double irony.

His body with its long legs was not awkward or ill-coordinated. But, I think owing to nervous tension building up within, he was given to sudden, large spasmodic movements. On the low seat of the famous yellow silk sofa he would sit with angled knees twisted to one side, very still until, abruptly, he would swing them across to the other side. Or occasionally he would shoot his body forward, letting his arms hang down to the floor, a picture of ironical despair.

When he was listening to music, these nervous movements died away and he sat quietly absorbed. His eyes seemed to look inwards, unless, at some favourite passage, he raised them to exchange a look of pure delight.

Life in the offices at Shire Hall was very different. His secretary, Mrs Dorothy Bimrose, remembers it like this:

From 9 o'clock till 9.30 there would be a sort of somnolence, a toying with the post, or a desultory rearrangement of files, but at about 9.35 someone would look out of the window and say: 'He's here', or 'His bicycle's in the rack', and backs would straighten, footsteps quicken and voices become quicker and more alert. Or the communicating door between Higher and Elementary would open and Mr T. would say 'The Great White Chief's in. Look out Mr H., he'll be after Elementary today. He tore me to *shreds* yesterday.' He might appear at the door and speak one's name, or simply beckon. Then he would lead the way along the corridor with his quick, light step which was somehow indicative of the verbal rapier thrusts that were to follow. The interview was invariably a masterly probing and pursuing through questioning until each cravenly concealed fault or inadequacy was brought to light. . . . and there were moments too of course that were memorable for the understanding shown and the sympathy indicated by a smile or a disarmed admission that he had been bully-ragging for too long.

He was by no means beloved by all his staff; the brother of one of them wrote: 'He was an awful liar. If things go right, H.M. did it; if wrong, the staff were to blame.' And Norman Fisher has described what he was like to work with:

Like many creative people Henry Morris was one whose nerve ends seem to have been nearer the surface than most. He was in consequence both moody and unpredictable. To work under him was at once fascinating and extremely exacting. . . . [34].[1]

One who remained devoted to him was George Hawes, his senior clerk, of whom Dorothy Bimrose has written:

George Hawes was a Yorkshireman, and the only one who dared bang Mr Morris's door. 'I've finished subscribing to Genius. That's the last time!' he'd say. But the next day he'd be working out a colour scheme with H.M. When Hawes died at the age of forty-six, Morris said: 'He was one of my best friends – my debt to him will never be repaid.'

The gap between his personal and his public life might seem to have been wide and maintained with care. But there were important links, and in many ways the one reflected and indeed nourished the other. His elegant, colourful flat; his concern that his table should be properly furnished, whether with silver and china or with food and wine; his near obsession with his own physical health and with tidiness; his delight in the countryside and with the arts and architecture – all these personal concerns penetrated his professional and public life. They animated the projects he developed and steered skilfully through committee, they informed the plans which he followed, hawklike, across the drawing boards until they emerged as colourful classrooms or distinguished buildings. Nor did he stop there; he would often appear unannounced at schools, at pains to keep them free from visual solecisms.

In effecting these links he was only following the line taken by all great teachers who are moved to share that which they love with those whom they teach. He went to unending trouble and often considerable personal expense to see that 'his' schools and village colleges were furnished with taste and provided, like his own home, with suitable works of art carefully selected. He would bring back pictures and pieces of sculpture from his holidays abroad and 'lend' them to schools. In 1954 he wrote to a friend: 'Would you have time after lunch to go with me to Kew Gardens in order to choose some green spheres (in box) for two of our village colleges. . . . I might also purchase one or two figures in box. As you know they are beautiful to look at and only have to be trimmed once a year.' There were always fresh flowers in his flat, and he was insistent that whenever possible flowers should be a part of school and classroom, but they had to be in vases or pots; never, but never, in jam jars. Children's art had its place, but this place was the classroom. Once, visiting a new village college he noticed in the entrance hall a display of pupils' paintings. He complained to the surprised Warden: 'You're making the place look like a school!' He was as concerned about weeds and litter as any park-keeper. He once sent a circular to all heads describing a scheme that

1 Numbers given in square brackets refer to the Bibliography at the end of the book.

he had come across at an independent school by which the litter problem had been solved.

He was always concerned that school dinners should be decorously served and partaken with some formality, for he said that the common meal had always played an important part in civilisation, claiming that it was 'one of the main instruments of education'. But he was equally keen that the food should both taste good and promote health. A domestic science organiser remembers her interview at Shire Hall, when he told her that once, when visiting a school, he had noticed one of the cooks in the school kitchen draining the boiled cabbage and allowing the water to go down the sink, instead of preserving it for soup: 'I bowed my head,' he told her, 'as if I had been at a funeral.'

He was almost obsessed with maintaining his own good health. 'How loathsome is illness and pain,' he once wrote, and had the Victorian masculine keenness on plenty of fresh air, fresh food and strenuous exercise. And he insisted that something should be done to make the children of Cambridgeshire healthy too. His first village college was to include a Health Wing, and he wrote enthusiastically about it: 'We shall begin with the expectant mothers, we shall pay special attention to the pre-school child . . . and we shall bridge the mischievous gap in the medical supervision of adolescents between fourteen and sixteen.'

He was a born teacher. Though he would not have known what to do when faced by a class of thirty children, the young men and women who came to know him in Cambridge, were, in a real sense, disciples. John Holloway (Fellow of Queens' and Professor of Modern English at Cambridge) expressed what many of us have felt, when he wrote: 'Henry was the most remarkable man I have ever known well. . . . Probably I owe him more, in terms of what I value in my own development, than I owe anyone else.'

He would go out of his way to enlist 'pupils' and then introduce them to the way he felt they should go. He urged them to read widely, to listen to music and immerse themselves in art. But he did more than urge. He knew how to communicate his own unique delight in a poem, a picture or a piece of music. One felt richer after being with him. John Holloway has noted not only this facility, but his ability to extend the aesthetic experience, and share it. 'He was marvellous in how closely, how genuinely he knew and communicated, that Mozart, wine, and making love could all come very close to each other.' He would introduce his 'pupils' to lively people. Above all he would encourage them to commit themselves to some career which served some worthwhile social purpose. He abhorred the wasted life.

In my first year at Cambridge, in 1933, I was given an introduction to him, in order to seek advice about a career in education. I went to see him in Shire Hall. I didn't think I made much impression, and as far as I was concerned the interview was not particularly memorable. But in the spring term of my third year, I was visiting an art exhibition when a tall man stopped near me and said: 'Are you still intending to go into education?' A little belatedly I recognised Morris and said, 'Yes'. Whereupon he invited me to call at his office the next day, and at this interview suggested that I should work there during the long vacation, in order to learn at first hand something about educational administration before I started at the Institute of Education in London, where I was going the following year to study for my teaching certificate.

When this little pre-apprenticeship experience at his office was over, I wrote to thank him, and sent him a copy of Duff Cooper's *Talleyrand* which had recently been published. For me the month had been enjoyable and useful. I had learned much, but his reply to my letter taught me more.

29 July '36

30A Trinity Street
Cambridge

Dear Harry,

Thank you very much for your charming and encouraging letter. I did not expect your stay in the office to be so successful, and so friendly in the best sense – which shows how difficult it is to form any reliable judgements until men are thrown together in extraverted interests (forgive my jargon). But I felt that you saw the *enormous* possibilities of education, even after seeing our moderate Cambridgeshire enterprises. I feel no complacency – only a daily dissatisfaction that so little is accomplished in a field so rich in possibilities.

I enjoyed your being here, and miss you: I inwardly appreciated your attitude very much and your being seized with the possibilities of the work, and I thought you showed much adaptability and ability in tackling such fragments of jobs we could give you to do. (Forgive any appearance of avuncular condescension.)

I hope you will deepen your knowledge of education in every kind of way and extract the utmost from the London Day Training College[1] – Please read as much as you can, and see as much as possible of good schools and teachers in Town.

I shall look forward to your coming to stay for a weekend next term, and to hearing from you in the meantime.

Gropius' revised plans for Histon are superb: a veritable architectural seduction, chaste and severe, but intense –

Ever yours
Henry

PS I was grateful for your book: and am reading it as an indulgence.

This was surely a good letter for a young man to receive. And he wrote many such letters to many people. They left their mark, not only because of the exhortations to which one responded, but because of the assumption of shared enthusiasms which all good teachers know how to make explicit. He spent his life teaching in this way.

1 The original name of the London University Institute of Education.

OBSCURE BEGINNINGS: 1889–1922

Morris was uncommunicative about his origins, about his family and about his life before Cambridge. Friends felt no inclination to break through the barrier which he set up around his past, and which he obviously preferred to maintain. A stranger once asked him what his father had been and where he had been to school and he told her that his father had been a solicitor, and that he himself had been educated privately. In the records of St David's, Lampeter, his father's profession is entered as an engineer. In his application for the post of Assistant Director of Education of Cambridgeshire, under the question relating to his schooling, he merely wrote: 'Privately, under Mr F. W. Jackson, M.A., Harris Institute, Preston, 1906–1910.'

In fact, his father was a Mr William Morris, a plumber, who brought up his large family in a small semi-detached house in Poulton Road, Southport. In the garden at the back were a few apple trees and some hen houses, for Mr Morris was a keen breeder of poultry, and once won the prize for a bantam cock at the Crystal Palace poultry show.

Henry was born on 13 November 1889, the seventh child of a family of eight. His mother was Irish, and had been a practising Roman Catholic until her marriage. She died when he was twelve. His older sisters then had to manage the house and look after the younger children, which they did with devotion. Like the rest of the family he went regularly to the parish church and Sunday school and attended the local elementary school. One of his elder brothers, Walter, remembers him there as a little boy who needed his protection, because Henry was rather frail and different from the other children; he early showed an interest in intellectual pursuits. 'I recall holding his hand wherever we went, and also getting into fights with other boys who wanted to make fun of Henry. At home he used to get the younger ones together and we'd be the congregation and he'd pretend to conduct a church service for us.' He remembers also expeditions with Henry to collect shells from the shore at Southport, and their helping their father grind them to make grit for his pullets; and how Henry hated cleaning out the hen houses and would try to get out of it.[1]

Henry left school at fourteen and got a job as office boy on the local paper, the *Southport Visitor*. Soon he began working there as a reporter and was so well thought of by the editor that he used to be given assignments which the older reporters thought should have been given to them. He came under the influence of Zechariah Edwards, the vicar of Crossens, a village a few miles from Southport. Henry took an active part organising the social life of the village church, including concerts in the church hall. His brother Walter recalls an

---

1 In later years, when exasperated by councillors or clerks he would sometimes say, 'I feel like an eagle in a hen house.' Was he recalling cleaning out his father's hen houses?

occasion when Henry secured the services of a well-known singer, and of his whispering to him during her performance: 'She's much too good for these villagers.' He played the piano at home, but almost always to himself. It was possibly the vicar who encouraged him to continue his education at the Harris Institute at Preston which had been founded in 1828 as the Preston Mechanics Institute and which had developed as a college providing a variety of courses for older students; he no doubt opened up for him the prospect of the priesthood and of full-time university education at St David's College, Lampeter.

He was almost 21 when he entered St David's, Lampeter in October 1910. St David's is even today an isolated academic outpost in the Welsh hills. It had been founded in 1827 as a theological college; it has recently become a fully constituent member of the University of Wales. When Morris went there in 1910 almost all the students were studying for their ordination and Morris himself was no exception. During one vacation from Lampeter he was invited to visit the Bishop of Carlisle, who no doubt wanted to keep in touch with young ordinands. Walter vividly recalls Henry's delight and surprise after such a visit: 'D'you know, Walter, when I arrived at the station, the Bishop was there to meet me, and he insisted on carrying my bags.' Students at St David's could take the first part of an Oxford degree from there and Morris availed himself of this opportunity. In 1912 he was awarded a second class in Theology Moderations of the University of Oxford, and moved on to complete his degree at Exeter College, Oxford.

He must have been glad to scrape the mud of the Welsh hills from his boots, for his last days at Lampeter were stormy. A minute of a meeting of the College Board, dated 26 June 1912, reads:

It was agreed, Professor Green dissenting, that Mr H. Morris, who had taken a disciplinary matter before the magistrates *proprio motu* and had failed to win his case, should be required to sign the following apology: 'I hereby express my sincere regret in regard to my recent action in taking matters of college discipline into the Law Courts without consulting the authorities of the college, so disregarding the method constitutionally provided for dealing with such questions and violating the universal tradition of corporate college life.'

This clash with authority began in May 1912 when the Principal of Lampeter, Dr Bebb, posted on the official college notice board a letter from him inviting students to sign a petition against the Welsh Disestablishment Bill which was about to be presented to Parliament. The effect of the Bill, if it had been passed, would have been to deprive the Anglican Church in Wales (and Lampeter College) of lands and property. On 27 May, a letter signed 'Lampeter Student' appeared in the *South Wales Daily News*, deploring the Principal's action, and suggesting that coercion to sign the petition had taken place. The next day the Principal called the whole college together and suggested that the students themselves would know how to deal with the cowardly writer of the anonymous letter. Thereupon the student president summoned all students to a meeting the following day, when he called upon those who had had nothing to do with the offending letter to stand up. Henry Morris and one other student called Roberts objected. In the course of the angry discussion, Morris was reported (in the *Western Mail* of 1 June) as stating 'that students at the college were not tied to any religious or political creed and that no interference with a man's opinions should be tolerated'.

Morris was interviewed by the *South Wales Daily News* and gave his story of subsequent events:

After the meeting broke up, Mr Roberts and myself were making our way through the corridor when we were hustled and struck, and we were both challenged to fight. When we got into the 'quad' the demonstration became more threatening, and, fearing we might be 'tanked', we made a rush to the Censor's house. . . . Professor Green went out and threatened the students with various penalties. Later in the day I took out summonses against six of the students for assault.

A hot exchange of letters was published in the local press; leading articles referred to 'Lampeter being the rendez-vous of curious scenes'; public meetings were called. Further letters from 'Lampeter Student' cast doubt, not only on the propriety of the Principal's action, but on the 'so-called university' status of Lampeter. In a final letter Dr Bebb stated that his petition had now been signed 'by all but one of the students at St David's'. This brought a swift reply on 6 June. 'Why tell us with a flourish of trumpets that the men under his charge have now come into line – all but one? What was the matter before?' This letter is signed 'Oxonian'. No doubt 'Lampeter Student' had already been accepted by Exeter College. There is no record of his ever having signed the apology.

He was deeply moved by Oxford; all his life he looked on its architecture with an almost sensual delight, and there he seems to have first felt the deeper joys of friendship. His tutor was Hastings Rashdall, celebrated historical scholar, author of *Universities of Europe in the Middle Ages*, the standard work on the medieval universities. He came to know Rashdall well, used to go and stay with him, and always referred to him with the greatest respect. Rashdall's picture of the ancient European universities, living communities of dedicated men enlightening a dark world and pursuing truth as they saw it, remained with Morris as an educational ideal to be upheld. But, as Rashdall wrote at the end of the final chapter of his book: 'Personal contact adds something even to the highest spiritual and intellectual influences, and it adds life and power to the teaching of man, whose books by themselves would be of comparatively small account.' These words are of particular significance in connection with Morris, for while he published little, he inspired a host of disciples by his personal contact and by his conversation and letters.

He recalled his prewar days at Oxford in a letter to Charles Fenn written twenty years later (May 1934), after a brief visit: 'Oxford looked magnificent. Great and gracious city. I went round and saw my former rooms and thought of the golden hours there years ago, and all my dear friends . . . killed in the war. We are all under sentence of death.'

By November 1914 he had joined up, and was posted to the Inns of Court O.T.C. and was later commissioned in the Royal Army Service Corps. He served as supply officer to the 41st Division, and was a staff officer with the 14th Corps in Italy from 1915 to 1919. He reached the rank of captain, and was mentioned in despatches. No doubt for him, as for many young men who had not been to Public Schools but who became officers during the first world war, his commission, and the experience it afforded him, opened doors for him in the postwar world, which otherwise would have had to be forced. As an officer in the R.A.S.C. he learned how to deal effectively with administrative responsibilities, and also, perhaps more important, to exercise responsibility according to the accepted English mode of leadership. He was a fast learner, and by the time he emerged from the army he had adopted the gestures and tone of voice of a successful public school product. His elementary school, the *Southport Visitor*, and St David's, Lampeter, could fade from his conversation, if not from his consciousness.

The war itself was another episode about which he seldom spoke. Strangely enough a framed photograph of himself as a young officer stood on a table in his sitting room until well into the thirties (see plate X).[1] When he did mention the war, it was to recall either the stupidities of regular officers or the lewdities of sergeants. He took a delight in both: the adjutant hoping earnestly for the war to end so that then they could get back 'to real soldiering'; the sergeant's goodnight advice to the barrack room: 'Slow mastication (*sic*) is the secret of long life – you lot ought to be issued with barbed wire gloves!' But his silence about 'the pity of war' surely hid some searing experiences; apart from the loss of friends, he knew the trenches and the horrors of the front. Once during his last days in 1961, delirious in hospital, he was heard to say: 'I've seen men hanging on the wire.'

When he was demobilised in 1919 he needed one more year at university to complete his degree. After a brief return to Oxford he decided not to stay there, where memories would have been piercing. He had definitely decided by then not to enter the Church. He applied to read philosophy at King's College, Cambridge. He was accepted, stayed four terms and was awarded an Upper Second in Part I of the Moral Science Tripos. At Cambridge he made many friends, and used to go on walking tours and motor trips with them. One of these,

1 From photographs 1 and 2 one can see clearly what the First World War experience did to the callow young student from Lampeter.

Keith Innes, who later became Chief Education Officer of Wiltshire, has written: 'The spirit of Oxford hung around him. Through him, I met his very lovable and scholarly friend, Canon Rashdall, whose kindness and wisdom enlarged my horizon. . . . I owed much to Henry in those days.'

From Cambridge he went to become a 'learner' in the Kent Education Offices. Here E. Salter Davies, the Director of Education, had started a scheme to introduce selected young men to educational administration in the local authority service. Morris, who was later, from his own office, to develop informally a similar scheme, was one of the first of the distinguished team who passed through Salter Davies's hands at Maidstone. There followed him Martin Wilson who became Chief Education Officer of Shropshire: 'I experienced the shockwave of his sojourn there'; R. N. Armfelt who became Chief Education Officer of Devon; John Trevelyan, later Sir John Trevelyan, who became Chief Education Officer of Westmorland; Robert Beloe, later Sir Robert Beloe, who became Chief Education Officer of Surrey; and Philip Morris, later Sir Philip Morris, who, succeeding Salter Davies, became Chief Education Officer of Kent. Of this impressive group, Henry Morris was the first to become chief officer of a local education authority. In 1921 he moved back to Cambridge to be Assistant Secretary for Education in the County Offices. After his chief's death in 1922, he succeeded as County Education Secretary; (in modern language, Chief Education Officer). He was 33.

When I came here [he said in a speech to Cambridgeshire teachers in 1946], I found a small informal office . . . a kind of bird's nest in Trinity Street. There was an air of leisure, of delayed and not too urgent decision, of truly antique office methods which, as I look back on it today, seems like a fairyland or as someone has said of the residential part of Oxford: 'a place where it is always Sunday afternoon'. After that, and I fear when I became Chief Education Officer, the dread hand of so-called reform began to have an influence.

Morris was now set for thirty-two almost unbroken years directing the education of a poor, small county, during which time he set up in it a model of educational development for all the world to see, to appraise, and (often without acknowledgement) to imitate.

2 THE IDEAS

Two motives made Morris a reformer. First a set of ideals based on religion, science, education and the arts; secondly the experiences of his childhood and youth. When he went, at the age of twenty, to St David's Lampeter, ordination was his goal. By the time he returned from the war, at the age of thirty, he had become an agnostic and a career in the Church was no longer conceivable. And yet religion held him till the end of his life. There was never a time when he did not delight in the outward forms of the Christian ritual, in church music and in the language of the Prayer Book and the Bible. Before going to Lampeter, besides his close connection with the parish church at Crossens, he used to enjoy reading the lessons in the church at Parbold, near Southport, where one of his elder sisters lived; and when he was working at Maidstone, immediately after coming down from Cambridge, he lodged with the rector of Hollingbourne and there also read the lessons in the church. Biblical quotations decorate his writing and often unexpectedly punctuated his speech. 'Smite the Philistines hip and thigh' he urged a young clerk at the Cambridge City Library, who, in spite of his committee, had succeeded in getting a number of high quality books on the shelves.

Church services well performed always moved him. I myself have known him sit rapt and entranced in a cold and almost empty Florentine church while a priest sang mass, and urchins played around the chancel steps, unheeding and unheeded. He would quite often attend evensong at King's or break into an afternoon's work at Shire Hall and get himself driven to Ely to hear a service there. The stress and speed of life made him value all the more what is hallowed and sacred, he liked to use the word 'numinous', and he insisted on the architect's obligation to recreate for future generations 'the numinous, that sense of awe, to create which is one of the main functions of architecture' [20]. When planning his village colleges and when writing later of the need in towns to build community centres where people could pass their time learning and living, reading and playing, eating and drinking, he wrote: 'And I would myself include places for worship, silence and meditation, where the sense of the sacred and eternal could be nourished' [20].

Thus, while religion in its widest and deepest sense meant much to him, his attachment to the doctrine of the church was severed, partly no doubt as a result of his war experience and partly too by the teachings of scientific humanism, which he must have taken in while studying contemporary philosophy at Cambridge. He linked science with education and put his faith in both:

We should expel all concepts which derive from a magical view of man and the universe. Until we have the courage to proceed undeviatingly from the point of view of a rationalist positivism, the articulation of a modern philosophy of education is impossible. The majority of people under forty know which view must prevail. When the scientific, realist outlook becomes dominant, then education . . . will become as exciting as war, and perhaps . . . its moral equivalent. The integration of modern communities is likely to come about by organising them around their educational institutions. Education thus conceived will be . . . the application of science and art to the life of the individual and society [4].

And so we come to the fourth source of his inspiration. The arts remained, throughout his life, a form of nourishment without which he would have starved. Literature, especially poetry, was his first master. He was not especially well-read, but he was intimately familiar with the works of a few chosen poets. John Holloway has pointed out, in this connection, 'how much he did, on so little. How few poems or paintings he was actually familiar with. Yet those he did know filled him with unique, and uniquely communicable, delight.' 'The whole of Keats vibrates for me', he wrote once to a friend. Wordsworth held him, and also Meredith, a copy of whose poems went with him through the war. Both of these combine a strong and optimistic moral sense with a deep sensitivity to nature, a combination which exactly suited his own outlook and inclination. A verse from Meredith's 'The Thrush in February' is inscribed on a plaque at the entrance to Impington Village College, the last line of which he liked to quote:

> Full lasting is the song, though he
> The singer passes: lasting too,
> For souls not lent in usury,
> The rapture of the forward view.

Goethe's *Faust* with its social and personal message meant much to him; Shakespeare's tragedies and Mozart's operas and chamber music enthralled him. Monteverdi he loved, and Brahms. Sometimes at Christmas he would organise a programme of readings and music in his house: Milton's 'Ode to the Nativity', Eliot's 'Journey of the Magi', Bach's Christmas Oratorio. He would lie back in his chair, and suddenly during a pause, stand up and strike an attitude of mock adoration, clasping the record he was about to put on, his eyes upturned in parody of a medieval saint. He was not unaware of the deficiency of musical reproduction before the days of LPs, and once referred to his radiogram playing Mozart's *Sinfonia Concertante* as a celestial barrel-organ.

He came later to painting and sculpture. Architecture he prized above all, perhaps because here science and art were linked and because architecture contributed, both socially and aesthetically, to the quality of life. He described it once as the best means we have of instituting compulsory aesthetic education. Hence the overriding importance for him of fine architecture for school buildings, and for good furniture, carefully chosen pictures, sculpture and gay colours inside the schools. And with this concern went the urge, which he believed should be felt by all with a responsibility for education, to encourage, by all possible means, and for people of all ages, what he called 'the consumption and production of art'.

Religion, education, science and the arts were then the chief sources of his inspiration; the power and meaning of each he transformed so that they generated in his mind particular and original and, above all, potent ideas. Potent because he had no use for what he called 'the sensuality of the idea'. With him the word had to become flesh. He was a planner, a committed planner, who could not rest while his plans remained unimplemented. He knew and admired Sidney and Beatrice Webb, and was a personal friend of G. D. H. Cole. His own copy of Cole's *Social Theory*, bought in 1924, is vigorously annotated.[1] But he despised the otiose intellectuals of London and Oxbridge, Bloomsburyites, Sunday paper journalists, belles-lettristes or half dead dons, 'hot air merchants' he called them, who could live off a diet of unapplied lucubrations. He could not, therefore, wait. 'Education' he would say 'is committed to the idea that the ideal order and the actual order can ultimately be made one.' This was the faith which he lived to prove.

These four impulses were basic; they drove him through his career as a public servant. Two further forces must be mentioned. First a binding loyalty to local government, and secondly an active and almost Victorian social conscience. These kept him working for twenty-five years with a small staff, in a small office, in a small county; kept him too from seeking and sometimes from accepting offers of much bigger things. In March 1924 John Reith (later Lord Reith) offered him a place at the top of the BBC hierarchy, supervising the education policy of the Corporation. The proposed salary was £2000. His own salary at the time was £600. He turned down the offer and explained to Reith that he felt he could be more effective working from a local government office rather than from a high and seemingly powerful central position.

During his early years as an administrator he saw to it that his ideas were known to the planners in the Labour Party. He contacted Arthur Henderson (Junior) when the latter was visiting Cambridge; Hender-

1 See page 34.

son was Assistant Secretary of the party Research Group and General Staff. He put to him the importance of 'friends of education' concentrating on the LEAs. He was subsequently asked by Henderson to write a memorandum, which would be entirely confidential, on the question of recruitment of local authority staff.

A clue to the strength and origin of his social conscience is contained in a Meredith poem 'The Empty Purse', and especially in a short excerpt from it which he had printed in the programme of one of his Festival Teachers' courses held at Sawston in 1951:

> Thou under stress of the strife
> Shalt hear for sustainment supreme
> The cry of the conscience of Life:
> Keep the young generations in hail,
> And bequeath them no tumbled house.

Until his death he kept the young generations in hail, and 'The cry of the conscience of Life' allowed him little rest: it impelled him to become a brilliant exponent of the art of the possible, a brilliant 'politician' and a creative administrator. Thus he not only despised unapplied musings of the purely doctinaire politician or dreamer, but also scathingly condemned the ineffectual fanaticism of the ideological revolutionary who is determined to remain pure even at the price of impotence. Here is he writing in 1936 to Charles Fenn who was moving far to the left as a result of the Spanish Civil War:

I am with you in your feelings about the Left. But I am afraid of all attitudes motivated too much by mere anger. I feel passionately the need for the uttermost reconstruction of human society. Ultimately, if we are to have a genuinely human civilisation, we must build on persuasion and education – the educational society. . . . We should remind ourselves that the only way is to begin afresh at training the young in thought and reflection – the middleaged are too far gone for that.

And I do not want a political programme to be based in a too fanatical deference to some past figure like Marx or anybody else – it must be an evolutionary doctrine capable of being developed in the light of experience and the contributions of contemporary genius. In politics we do not want fanaticism and irrationalism and lunging emotion (most of it neurasthenic). Let us depend on reason and science and art and on will and imagination and integrity of mind.

And in a further letter, a fortnight later, he returned to the theme; unable to resist holding up his own practical approach as a far better model for a young man to follow:

Do, I pray you, keep free of ideological and minority fanaticism. Infinite harm, not to be measured, is done by antipathetic emotion generated by sectional exclusiveness. It is the universal method of getting up spurious steam. The Etonian has it; the 'County' has it; . . . university men put it across non university men; . . . people in the suburbs become freemasons in order to feel that they have some minority privileges that others are shut out of. Your evangelical revolutionaries are playing the same old game, building up a sense of superiority on some principle of exclusion.

I am for the scientific commonwealth, devoid of fanaticism and irrational anger and eructation.

As to being constructively communal in the belief that only a communal world order, in which every single being is significated in the economic and cultural order, I can equal you any day, and I work at it every day, and at nothing else.

But alongside the influences already mentioned – his interest in religion, education, science and the arts, the influence of poets, philosophers and political scientists, his social conscience connected with his firm belief in local government and pragmatism – there lies, undoubtedly, the influence of his own personal experiences as a boy and as a young man. His brother Walter confirms that his childhood in his large family was marked by affectionate care, which continued undiminished after his mother died, when his two elder sisters ran the house. On the other hand, his elementary schooling can have given him neither joy nor nourishment, for it was short and according to his brother, brutish. His time on the *Southport Visitor*, and his experience organising social events for the vicar of Crossons, introduced him to the small world of local dramatic societies, choirs and clubs: seed beds of indigenous collective initiative. His early attachment to the Church was real, but the Lampeter experience was obviously not happy and by the end of his time there he was close to despising the college. It was an undistinguished, insulated community and he soon came to dislike and disapprove of this element of insularity. On the other hand Oxford and then Cambridge captivated him, as they have so often captivated young men coming to them from obscure origins. He saw weak points, and spoke with undisguised disdain of the average don. But his attachment to the pure essence of the university ideal, which he learned no doubt from Rashdall, was indestructible, for in Oxford and Cambridge he discovered himself, and there he saw culture successfully resisting anarchy.

All these experiences seem to have engendered theories and ideas which later were to be embodied in the idea of the village college. In the *Memorandum* of 1924 on village colleges [Appendix XIV] he wrote: 'Has there ever been an educational institution that provided for the needs of the family and consolidated its life?' But the projected village college would not only contribute to family life, it would open up opportunities for the enrichment of the lives of the whole population of a large rural area, 'a community centre for the neighbourhood', he called it. For unlike 'non-local' residential institutions, such as the public schools or Lampeter, it would not be insulated from the lives of those who lived around it. On the other hand, from the university ideal the village college would take the inter-

See pages 15–16.

Part of letter Henry Morris wrote to Charles Fenn on 1st December 1936.

weaving of study with recreation, the mixing of intellectual with physical nourishment, and the establishment of a corporate unit where wide diversity of interests and activities would be fostered. But it would avoid the intellectual and social exclusiveness of the universities.

Finally, and no doubt this sprang from his lean years of compulsory schooling, he was to see the need for a complete metamorphosis of the school experience, particularly for the huge majority of children who were not going to grammar school. This he suggested should be effected in two ways. First, 'we must shift the bias of education from childhood to youth and maturity'; then teachers would no longer feel impelled forcibly to feed the young with material which only an older person could be expected to assimilate. Secondly he insisted that endless 'didactic discourse' in classrooms be replaced by creative activity. Here he was speaking for the largely voiceless majority (with whom he had shared classrooms at school in Southport) for whom intellectual concentration, divorced from the world outside and from practical activity, was almost impossible. To overcome the tendency of teachers to expect too much of the young too soon he gave permanent education a base in the village college. At the same time he broke through the barriers of the 'traditional school', opening doors and windows to the local community, and, as a logical consequence, encouraged the development of practical subjects and 'vocational' experience to children at school, as well as to young people and adults.

Thus he shifted the bias of education both in time and in content. Greater emphasis than before was to be placed on artistic pursuits, and on crafts which had a vocational connection. In this he established in Cambridgeshire a pattern of schooling for the 'average child' long before the latter appeared in the pages of the Newsom Report of 1963.

CONCEPTION OF THE VILLAGE COLLEGE

After he left Oxford Morris kept in touch with his tutor, Hastings Rashdall, who remained an influence throughout his life and one he liked to acknowledge. Rashdall had introduced him to the golden age of European Catholicism when the all powerful Church had lent a unity to social as well as to spiritual life. But Morris looked back on this lost world without any intention of rebuilding it. In an article in the *New Ideals Quarterly* in March 1926, he wrote:

I do not think we can look forward to the arising of another great all-embracing religious organisation like the Catholic Church that will assemble and marshall the temporal order of society under the sanctions of eternity, thus redeeming the episode of life on one of the humblest of the planets from triviality, ruin and despair. Much less . . . can we hope or wish that we should be saved by the device of the worship of the visible state, whether conceived in Germany or elsewhere [3].

He proceeded, in the same article, to compare the pervasive contribution made by the Catholic Church to education in its widest sense, with the derisible part played by the Church of England in the foundation of a system of state education. On the one hand there towered a great religious organisation which 'nourished a civilisation' and whose cultural influence extended far beyond the education of the young, or of any one section of the community, and on the other there was the Church of England with its National Society for the Education of the Poor in the Principles of the Established Church. Its puny contribution, he suggested, explained the 'profound futility' of our state system of education, which was built on foundations laid down by the National Society.

He saw clearly that there could be no return to the pre-industrial world even though he recognised that this world had offered people life-giving satisfactions of which contemporary man, especially urban man, was often deprived – in particular the assurances that he was a significant and contributing member of his community. But the urban explosion of the nineteenth century and new methods of production and transport had destroyed the primitive scene, whether it was in Nottingham or (as he was later to recognise) in Nigeria, and to it there was no return.

Everywhere the cloud of technology, though big with material blessings for millions, was also blotting out the light which once emanated from primitive arts, and traditional communal customs. At the same time, clear-cut religious beliefs and well defined sanctions were becoming blurred, obscured and even forgotten. He pointed to the failure in cities and the countryside to achieve an 'art of living': 'Walk through a city on a Saturday night, or through a country town or village and see for yourselves how little our state system of education is doing to help the multitudes to live a life worth living, or even enjoy their leisure' [3].

But he refused to be dismayed. We needed first to meet the threatening cultural calamity with rebuilt educational defences, and then to bend the technological revolution to serve our own carefully thought out ends. And in confronting the new and more difficult problems which were bearing down on us, he not only expounded a solution, but, through administrative and political skill, he realised this solution in bricks and glass and steel, in the village colleges of Cambridgeshire.

Morris pinned his faith on education, and added two essentials. First, we must plan: he insisted that the vision of planners should extend to a far wider horizon than was usual. They should be concerned not merely with economic efficiency, not merely with sewers and roads and housing, but with the total social scene. This newly planned environment should therefore serve cultural as well as educational and economic ends. Secondly we must reconstruct our conception of education 'so that it will be co-terminous with life'.

At the present moment our state system of education is concerned almost wholly with children and the teachers of children. We ought to see our way to the organic provision of education for the whole adult community. We must do away with the insulated school. We must so organise the educational buildings of the towns and countryside that the schools of the young are either organically related to, or form part of, the institutions in which the ultimate goals of education are realised. We must associate with education all those activities which go to make a full life – art, literature, music, festivals, local government, politics. This is as important for the teaching of the young, as it is for the teachers themselves. . . . It is only in a world where education is confined to infants and adolescents that the teacher is inclined to become a pundit or a tyrant.

We should picture a town or village clustering around its educational buildings, with its hall, library, and recreation grounds, where young and old not only acquire knowledge but are inducted into a way of life. . . .

We should abolish the barriers which separate education from all those activities which make up adult living . . . it should be the first duty of education to concern itself with the ultimate goals of education. . . . Man's life as an economic, social and religious animal – that is the subject matter of education and education the means whereby he achieves the best in all these respects. . . . It is the life the adult will lead, the working philosophy by which he will live, the politics of the community which he will serve in his maturity that should be the main concern of education [3].

And just as he was well aware that neither the medieval nor the primitive ideal could be reconstructed for the use of twentieth-century man, so he came to realise that salvation was not to be found in transplants from abroad. The suggestion has sometimes been made that the Danish Folk High School had served as a model for the village colleges [38]. He denied this specifically on at least two occasions. In 1924, in the *Memorandum* promoting the village colleges, he made the point quite clearly:

Unlike non-local residential institutions (the Public Schools, the Universities, a few residential working men's colleges, or, to take a foreign example, the Danish Folk High Schools), the Village College would not be divorced from the normal environment of those who would frequent it from day to day, or from the greater educational institution, the family. [See Appendix XIV.]

In later years a too frequent repetition of the charge of plagiarising the Danish experiment may have pricked him on to write an article for *Adult Education* of December 1941: it has the significant title, 'The Danish Folk High School Myth'. In this piece he sets out to show how radically even the aims of the Danish Folk High School differed from the real achievements of the village college. He maintained that the former was established largely to remedy the defects of the Danish elementary school and that the high school syllabus remained elementary, tied to the inculcation of Danish culture without technical instruction of any kind. The Folk High School was therefore a palliative, and separate from normal life. 'To provide resident hostels in the countryside to which a minority may escape, at infrequent intervals, the squalor and frustration of the contemporary town, does not begin to deal with the cultural needs of modern communities.' He concluded that the folk high school had largely outlived its function and asked: 'Does the Danish Folk High School indicate any of the methods by which we can provide the right kind of education for the English countryside? My answer is: "Absolutely no".'

He was planning to provide the framework and foundation for a local indigenous institution, a cultural focal point for the multifarious activities of a normal neighbourhood giving opportunities for the free development of ideas and of social groups.

The welfare of communities [he wrote], and the vigour and prosperity of their social life depend on the extent to which centres of unfettered initiative can be developed within them. The great task of education is to convert society into a series of cultural communities . . . where every local community would become an education society, and education would not merely be a consequence of good government, but good government a consequence of education [3].

Clearly, and for an administrator surprisingly, Morris was thinking out afresh the aims of civilisation; in doing so he not only induced others to do so too, he also set about applying his prescriptions in the only place where he had the power to do so, in his own county.

So, for the first time in the history of English education, the chief officer of a local education committee devised for his county a plan which he saw as having universal significance. He would establish a chain of institutions which would bring new life to areas which until then had been barren and underdeveloped. He was concerned not merely with the schooling of children, but with the cultural, recreational and economic life of the whole population.

He saw Cambridgeshire as an ideal 'demonstration area' for his experiment because it was so backward. The soil, it is true, was fertile, but in the 1920s agriculture everywhere had slumped and the countryside was blighted and abandoned. The squireless villages, the farms and the little schools all showed signs of poverty and neglect. Most of the schools were provided by the Church of England, some by the Free Churches. Little money was available for upkeep and repair. Not only were the schools in inadequate and out of date buildings, most of them were far too small to be able to offer a wide school experience to children who stayed there from the age of five till they left at fourteen. Many of these schools had only two teachers; schools with only one teacher were not uncommon. Out of a total of 134 in the county, only twenty-one had over a hundred children on the register. The older boys and girls were often left to look after themselves, marking time at school and waiting for that birthday which would ensure their end of term release. This picture is confirmed by

John Parr, who became the first Warden of Impington in 1939. He started his career in Cambridgeshire in 1925, attracted by what he read of Morris's plans. He describes his first village school, at Balsham, a few miles from Linton:

The population of Balsham had fallen from 1700 to 800. Agriculture was the main source of employment and wages were low. A few men worked outside the village. Girls found employment in domestic work. A bus ran to Cambridge twice a week. The village had no electricity or gas, no main drainage and the water came from two deep wells at each end of the village. . . . The school was all-age, 5 to 14 years with about 120 on roll, divided into four classes. Woodwork and cookery were taught in the Church Institute; benches were carried in and put away at each lesson.

The problem was not confined to Cambridgeshire, it was a national one. What Morris set out to do was radically to reform rural education, so that the standards of schools and of schooling offered to country children, and the opportunities for continuing education and for recreation offered to their parents, should equal or be better than what was offered the people of the towns. Many people were pessimistic about what could be done. On 13 December 1924 a leading article in *The Times Educational Supplement* protested:

The rural problem is one that successive governments have ignored in despair. The elementary school buildings are inadequate and insanitary in an appalling proportion of cases; the lack of facilities for continued and secondary education is a disgrace to a highly organised community. All the necessary things can be done. What we wish to emphasise is that they are not being done, and they do not seem likely to be done.

When he took over in Cambridgeshire in 1922 Henry Morris decided that the time had come for the necessary things to be done. He would attack this national problem. His solution was to put an end to the cultural stagnation of the countryside, and so arrest the flow of talent to the big towns. To this end he would plan a system of child and adult education for Cambridgeshire which would form a network of 'rural regions' and concentrate educational and cultural resources in the big villages and country towns, thus making them attractive to live and work in, and thereby retaining and reinvigorating the population. He saw salvation for the countryside only if the rural region could be given the potential (which the village lacked) to compete with the magnetism of the town.

He planned his campaign with the meticulous care of a military commander. Having determined his objectives, he proceeded to make an appraisal of the local situation. He noted that the town of Cambridge attracted the more adventurous young men and women of the fen villages. The country people came in to Cambridge for entertainment – for cinemas, dances and company; they came to find work; they came for evening classes. Some moved in for good, since Cambridge offered better houses, better wages and better schools. The cleverest children from the villages were drawn in, by scholarships, to the town grammar schools where the education they received did nothing to induce them to return and settle in their villages. They had, as he said, been 'lost to the towns'.

In the villages there was nothing to hold them. Tinkering with existing schools would do nothing to solve the problem. The rot would only be stopped by creating new institutions which not only provided a full range of secondary education but also served the needs of the adult population of the region. To launch immediately a full scale campaign to achieve this end was out of the question. A cluster of obstacles lay ahead of him which would have to be destroyed or neutralised before he launched his main attack. These obstacles were the small, 'all-age' Church schools, which in Cambridgeshire outnumbered the County Schools by three to one.[1] Before establishing

---

1 Church schools are so called because they were founded and are partly financed

his new 'county' secondary schools at strategic central points, he would have to persuade the managers of these Church schools either to vote their school out of existence or to release their older children, after they became eleven years old, to go to his new county secondary schools, where the churches had no special power over staff appointments or religious instruction. He was entering a minefield. Memories of previous long-drawn-out battles between Church and State over elementary schooling were still fresh.

His plan was to get the Church and the Chapel authorities to help him devise a syllabus of religious instruction which would, by agreement, be followed in all the county schools of Cambridgeshire. If the religious bodies found that the resulting syllabus was acceptable, they would agree to children being transferred to county schools who might otherwise attend their schools. Morris could then organise senior schools large enough to warrant their forming the nucleus of a still larger educational unit serving the adult population as well, thus becoming the basis for a village college.

THE CAMBRIDGESHIRE SYLLABUS

The members of the committee which was to draw up the Agreed Syllabus of Religious Instruction were selected with great care and diplomacy. The people themselves were less important than the offices they held. The Chairman was the Vice-Chancellor of the University, The Reverend E. C. Pearce, D.D., Master of Corpus Christi College and a member of the Cambridgeshire Education Committee; the other members who accepted the Vice-Chancellor's invitation to join him were:

The Regius Professor of Theology and Fellow of Jesus College,
    the Rev. A. Nairne, D.D.
The Master of St Catherine's College,
    the Rt. Rev. Bishop T. W. Drury, D.D.
A Fellow of Peterhouse,
    the Rev. G. H. Clayton, M.A.
The Principal of Mansfield College, Oxford,
    the Rev. W. B. Selbie, D.D.
The Public Orator and Fellow of St John's College,
    the Rev. T. R. Glover, M.A.
The President of Cheshunt College,
    the Rev. S. Cave, D.D.
The Professor of New Testament Theology, Westminster College,
    the Rev. C. Anderson Scott, D.D.
The Professor of Moral Philosophy and Fellow of King's College,
    W. R. Sorley, Litt.D.

by funds raised by religious denominations. A majority of the managers or governors is nominated by the churches. County schools are financed entirely from public funds – from rates and taxes.

The Professor of English Literature and Fellow of Jesus College,
  Sir Arthur Quiller-Couch.
  There were also two headmasters, George Sampson of the Marl-
borough School, Chelsea, and J. Arrowsmith of Burwell Senior
School, Cambridgeshire; a headmistress, Miss Lowe of the Leeds High
School; and the principal of a training college, Miss Mercier of
Whitelands. There were two Assessors: the Rev. G. W. Evans,
Canon Residentiary of Ely (Secretary of the Ely Association of
Voluntary Schools), and J. C. Isard, the Secretary of the Cambridge-
shire Federation of Free Churches.
  The Secretary: H. Morris.
  The report was published at the end of 1923. A short preface, signed
by Henry Morris, was quite open about the initial impetus behind it:

In order to facilitate the transfer of children from one type of school to
another or better still to secure a uniform system in the area by the transfer
of voluntary schools to the Authority, they (the Education Committee)
decided to take in hand the problem of providing an adequate and efficient
system of religious instruction for their area.

The introduction to the syllabus is written in a peculiar staccato
style. It is appropriately optimistic about the possibility of teaching
religion in schools, and while facing the difficulties and doubts felt by
all thinking Christians as a result of recent biblical criticism, it
expresses confidence that teachers were more than ready to take on
the task, and (striking a very modern note) that they would not do this
in an authoritarian manner.

The ambition of teachers is enlarged of late. No longer are they content to
impart information. They would give and take with pupils. . . . For in the
recent past Authority had given place to teaching, and today *teaching gives
place to conversation*. [My italics HAR.]
  The world is unhappy for lack of knowledge and schools are workshops
where the treasure of knowledge can be ordered by teachers and scholars at
real work together. They would launch at once into creative service.

An interesting distinction is made between theology and religion,
so that one wonders whether the anonymous author is not recalling
the shackles of Lampeter which he had long since shed. He writes:

Religion, the plain man's choice, is opposed sometimes to Theology, the
churchman's pedantry. If words matter, religion, which means awe or
obligation, seems less charming than theology which means learning about
God. The Day school, however is no place for creeds, prayer books, or the
masculine delicate and devotional precision of dogmatic religion. [My
italics HAR.]

Money is not mentioned in the report, but financial considerations
certainly weighed with the Cambridgeshire Education Committee.
This was freely admitted when the report came to be debated in the

council chamber. Already in one area of the county, at Burwell, by closing some of the small schools and by centralising the schooling of older children in the new senior school, important economies had been achieved, while at the same time educational standards had been raised [see paragraph V of *The Memorandum* (Appendix)]. But this reorganisation had only been possible because all the schools concerned were under the direct control of the local authority. The intention was to extend the policy, and the committee had therefore undertaken the task of devising an agreed syllabus of religious instruction, so that the Burwell pattern could be repeated anywhere in the county.

Backed both by financial and educational arguments, and supported by that heavy concentration of eminent divines and venerated Cambridge figures, the report could hardly be rejected by the education committee. It was in fact given an enthusiastic reception. A headline in the *Cambridge Chronicle* of 2 January 1924 announced: 'Dual Control Doomed' and the article underneath reflected both local pride and the almost euphoric atmosphere which seems to have gripped the council chamber on 1 January 1924.

'We believe that the Cambridgeshire Education Committee have achieved what parliament has from time to time ineffectually attempted.' The chairman congratulated the Vice-Chancellor's Committee on a syllabus 'which will become historic in the annals of public education not only for the reason that it is approved by high dignitaries of the Church of England and of the Free Churches, but also because it will unlock the gate which has hitherto barred the road to the single administration of all our schools'. On all sides there were hearty congratulations on what were termed the 'glorious results'. During the meeting of the education committee it was stated that representatives of the voluntary schools were so well satisfied that they were prepared to recommend the trustees (the managers) of the Church schools to hand over their schools to the local education authority. The Vice-Chancellor believed that

the standard of the elementary education was rising, largely due to the excellent idea of having senior schools; in order to make this universal they had to get rid of religious difficulties. Mr Morris saw a splendid vision and they were greatly indebted to him for the very successful realisation of that vision . . . and they must not forget the meed of thanks they owed to Mr Morris.

The national press also expressed approval. *The Times* of 2 January gave more than a column to the news, under the headline, 'Concordat at Cambridge', and *The Manchester Guardian* of the same date welcomed the publication of the syllabus in a leading article. But not everyone was happy. *The Church Times* of 25 January devoted a leader to the Cambridge Concordat:

It is very well meant . . . but taken as a whole it is more insidious and more dangerous than any of its predecessors. Unlike the Manchester scheme, which lies outside the fold of practical politics, the Cambridgeshire Concordat can be – and its champions propose that it shall be – put into operation at once.

The Church Times objected, of course, to the intimation that the Bible could be taught 'without reference to the doctrine of the Church'. It went on: 'We need not discuss this view, beyond remarking that every Church school in the land was built and is maintained as a protest against it.'

But there is no denying that Morris had done his work successfully and skilfully; his political skill is perhaps best seen in the order of priority in which the *Cambridge Daily News* (2 January 1924) arranged the various aspects of the plan, stressing first the financial, then the religious and finally the educational consequences.

How a saving of several thousands of pounds per year could be effected with regard to elementary education was described at a special meeting of the County Education Committee on Tuesday afternoon. Recommendations with regard to religious instruction were approved by the Committee and it was stated that as a result many Church schools were willing to be transferred to the Committee. If this course were to be adopted it would enable the Committee to see the entire fruition of their scheme for re-organising all the elementary schools in the county, and by so doing there would be a saving of £15,000 annually.

'The recommendations with regard to religious instruction' constituted in fact more than a syllabus for the teaching of scripture. *The Times* had been right to call it 'a religious concordat', and the chairman was justified in saying that it was 'historic'. This Cambridgeshire Syllabus of 1924 was the first one in the country to be agreed and acted upon. Some other education authorities composed their own, but the majority of education authorities in England were pleased to take over the Cambridgeshire Syllabus without alteration.

Morris, in one of his first major administrative acts had brought off a coup. But it was more than a tactical success. It is an early example of Morris the administrator energetically exercising political and diplomatic skill in order to advance his long-term ends, ends which even some of his committee were not aware of. He had succeeded by appealing to them partly as guardians of the public conscience in matters of religion, partly as keepers of the public purse, and partly as politicians pleased to be among the front runners, not merely in the solution of the religious question, but in the eventual implementation of a national system of separate senior and junior schools with a division at the age of eleven.

This reorganisation of elementary education was to be the principal recommendation of the Consultative Committee on Education Chairman: Lord Hadow), whose report, *The Education of the Adolescent* was published in 1926. Robert Logan, a lifelong friend of Morris, who became Chief Education Officer of Worcestershire once said: 'Henry's Cambridgeshire Syllabus made Hadow possible.'[1]

Looking back one can now see that Morris had taken advantage of, had even helped to bring about, one of those rare moments in history, when the first step towards reform can safely and easily be taken. This is when the immediate aims of the long-term reformer converge with the aims of the short-term realist, and each agrees on a single line of advance. Many of the councillors were not even aware of Morris's vision of a network of village colleges for Cambridgeshire. He himself did not share their concern with keeping down the rates, nor with their prestige. But they could work together in removing initial obstacles and Morris recognised that he could now move on and reveal his scheme for the village colleges.

THE MEMORANDUM

Robertson Scott was the Editor of *The Countryman* between the wars. He was a national figure, representing the nature-loving and slightly eccentric English gentleman. His book, *England's Green and Pleasant Land* (Cape, 1925) contains eulogistic references to Henry Morris and to the idea of the village college. He must have known Morris quite well, because in the summer of 1924, the latter spent a week at his home, Idebury Manor, near Kingham in Oxfordshire. In an annexe to the house Morris worked, putting the finishing touches to a short pamphlet he had written and was going to get published at his own expense by the Cambridge University Press. The pamphlet had a long title: *The Village College. Being a Memorandum on the Provision of Educational and Social Facilities for the Countryside, with Special Reference to Cambridgeshire*.

It was a seminal work. In twenty-four pages he introduced to the world, and to the county councillors of Cambridgeshire in particular, his plan for establishing a system of dynamic indigenous centres of education for the countryside, and in this instance for Cambridgeshire. The first edition which appeared in December 1924 was marked confidential, since he did not want publicity before the matter had been debated by the County Council. All councillors and aldermen therefore received a copy with their Christmas mail; it was sent also to the Board of Education and the Ministry of Agriculture, the Carnegie Trustees, the National Council of Social Service and the Development Commissioners.[2] Lord Hadow's committee also received a copy and the acknowledgement reported that the committee had 'decided to

1 Morris in fact anticipated the Hadow recommendations at Burwell; there is a graphic description of this pre-Hadow reorganisation in paragraph V of *The Memorandum*, p. 145.
2 These were grant-giving committee set up by the government towards the end of the war to encourage and finance constructive new schemes of postwar reconstruction.

consider the scheme in connection with the enquiry being conducted by them into post-primary education'.

The memorandum contains some of Morris's most effective public writing; it gives a clear picture of the factual and ideological background against which the village colleges were conceived, and shows his skill in projecting his ideals in energetic language and with a concern for detail. The full text is given in the Appendix: extensive quotations follow here;

If we wish to build up a rural civilisation that will have chronic vigour the first essential is that the countryside should have a localised and indigenous system of education in its own right, beginning with the child in the primary school.

The first step towards providing the countryside with a more efficient education will lie in the re-organisation of village schools into a system of Senior or Central schools in the larger villages, supported by tributary junior schools in the smaller surrounding villages.

But if rural England is to have the education it needs and the social and recreational life it deserves, more is required than the re-organisation of the elementary school system, and that which is required is possible. . . .

There must be a grouping and co-ordination of all the educational and social agencies which now exist in isolation in the countryside, an amalgamation which, while preserving the individuality and function of each, will assemble them into a whole and make possible their expression for the first time in a new institution, single but many-sided, for the countryside (III).

After pointing out that the County Council already possessed powers to provide 'educational, recreational and community facilities for the countryside' he went on to show that where these were provided, all too often they were separated, uncoordinated and inadequate. He gave as an example, the village branch of the county library, which was often housed in the corner of a school room or even in a private house. In a significant footnote, he drew attention to the 'almost universal need . . . for a room for reading during the long winter evenings, when the small cottage is filled by the family, and the light none too good for reading'.

In Cambridgeshire the aim would be to establish in about ten carefully selected centres, where Senior Schools are already organised, a system of village colleges which would provide for the co-ordination and development of all forms of education: primary, secondary, further and adult education, including agricultural education, together with social and recreational facilities, and at the same time, furnish a community centre for the neighbourhood . . . the narrower conception associated with the isolated elementary school would be abolished. It would be absorbed into the larger institution (X).

There followed a list of the opportunities and the facilities with details of the actual grounds, buildings and amenities which the village college could consist of: he enumerated fifteen items, including of course a library, an assembly hall and a staff room, (all these unknown in elementary schools), a nursery school, a clinic, and 'simple shower-baths and a dressing room, both in a basement, for the use of schoolchildren and of the Athletic Clubs of the village. Village athletes', he added, 'hardly ever enjoy the luxury of a hot bath and a rub down after the game.'

The government of the village college would be in the hands of a widely representative board of governors, while the head of the college would be a schoolmaster of distinction. 'An appropriate title expressing this new status and wider scope is therefore required. He might be styled "The Warden" . . . and why not Provost or Master or Principal in some cases?' (One can see not only in these suggested titles, but in the plea for shower baths for the village athletes, that in odd ways his model for the village college derived from the men's colleges of Oxford and Cambridge.)

He pointed out that the college would provide a meeting place and rich opportunities for existing or for newly formed voluntary associations. 'This would be the surest guarantee of their welfare and vigour. Without violence being done to freedom, some unity in the life of the rural community will be obtained.' (The use of the future, rather than the conditional tense here is significant.) When he reached the point where he began to describe the building itself, his intense interest and belief in Architecture in its widest sense, seemed to inspire his prose:

The building that will form the village college will be so new in English Architecture, and its significance so great, that the design and construction of the first village colleges should be very carefully provided for. For we are in measurable sight, if we use imagination and have administrative courage, of giving to the English countryside a number of fine and worthy public buildings. The schools of rural England are nearly always bad and seldom beautiful – never a form of art, as they might and ought to be. The greater proportion of them were designed to serve the joint purpose of a school and parish hall, and at a time when the standard of staffing and accommodation, the quality of the curriculum and the conception of teaching were vastly inferior to those of our own day.

As the Education Act of 1921 is progressively put into operation, the buildings are bound to be replaced. There is no reason why the erection of the new buildings should not be made the opportunity of adding to the public architecture of the countryside; and there is additional reason that the opportunity should not be missed because there is not likely ever to be any other constructive movement so national and widespread, so completely affecting the lives of the whole community, as that of public education. The provision of buildings for the system of public education will in the present century be one of the chiefest ways in which the art of architecture can influence the body politic. If the opportunity is not taken it will only be through dullness and lack of vision.

Using our imagination, let us say to the architect: 'Education is one of our greatest public services and one of the most widely diffused. Every year we spend on it some 80 millions. Every town and every village must have its educational buildings. Education touches every citizen. We have a conception of a new institution for the countryside, an institution that will touch every side of the life of the inhabitants of the district in which it is placed. Will you think out a design for such a building, a village college? A building that will express the spirit of the English countryside which it is intended to grace, something of its humaneness and modesty, something of the age-long and permanent dignity of husbandry; a building that will give the countryside a centre of reference arousing the affection and loyalty of the country child and country people, and conferring significance on their way of life? If this can be done simply and effectually, and if the varying needs which the village college will serve are realised as an entity and epitomised in a building, a standard may be set and a great tradition may be begun; in such a synthesis architecture will find a fresh and wide-spread means of expression. If the village college is a true and workable conception, the institution will, with various modifications, speed over rural England; and in course of time a new series of worthy public buildings will stand side by side with the parish churches of the country-side.' (XIII)

And so he came to his summing up:

The village college as thus outlined would not create something super-fluous; it would not be a spectacular experiment and a costly luxury. It would take all the various vital but isolated activities in village life – the School, the Village Hall and Reading Room, the Evening Classes, the Agricultural Education Courses, the Women's Institute, the British Legion, Boy Scouts and Girl Guides, the recreation ground, the branch of the County Rural Library, the Athletic and Recreation Clubs – and, bringing them together into relation, create a new institution for the English countryside. It would create out of discrete elements an organic whole; the vitality of the constituent elements would be preserved, and not des-troyed, but the unity they would form would be a new thing. For, as in the case of all organic unities, the whole is greater than the mere sum of the parts. It would be a true social synthesis – it would take existing and live elements and bring them into a new and unique relationship.

The village college would change the whole face of the problem of rural education. As the community centre of the neighbourhood it would provide for the whole man, and abolish the duality of education and ordinary life. It would not only be the training ground for the art of living, but the place in which life is lived, the environment of a genuine corporate life. The dismal dispute of vocational and non-vocational education would not arise in it. It would be a visible demonstration in stone[1] of the conti-nuity and never ceasingness of education. There would be no 'leaving school'! – the child would enter at three and leave the college only in extreme old age. It would have the great virtue of being local so that it would enhance the quality of actual life as it is lived from day to day – the supreme object of education. . . . Has there ever been an educational institution that at one and the same time provided for the needs of the whole family and consolidated its life – its social, physical, intellectual and economic life? Our modern educational institutions provide only for units

1 Once again one sees that the model college he had in mind was very closely related to Oxbridge.

of the family, or separate the individual from the family by time and space so that they may educate it apart and under less natural conditions. The village college would lie athwart the daily lives of the community it served; and in it the conditions would be realised under which education would be not an escape from reality, but an enrichment and transformation of it. For education is committed to the view that the ideal order and the actual order can ultimately be made one . . .

We are witnessing in this country, through the extension of the principle of ownership, the disappearance of the old land owning class. The responsibilities of leadership and the maintenance of liberal and humane traditions in our squireless villages (which are the rule not the exception in Cambridgeshire) will fall on a larger number of shoulders – they will fall on the whole community. The village college will be the seat and guardian of humane public traditions in the countryside, the training ground of a rural democracy realising its social and political duties. Without some such institution as the village college a rural community consisting largely of agricultural workers, small proprietors and small farmers will not be equal to the task of maintaining a worthy rural civilisation. Finally, the village college would not outlive its function, for the main reason that it would not be committed irrevocably to any intellectual or social dogma or to any sectional point of view. Intellectually it might be one of the freest of our English Institutions (XIV).

The final pages contain a 'Suggested Plan' for Cambridgeshire, locating ten village colleges, and proposing, at once, the establishment of two, at Sawston and at Bourne, as a pilot scheme. He was here appealing as much to the big charitable trusts and central government as to his own committee:

If the Carnegie Trustees and the Development Commissioners could father such a scheme, they might perform a work of reconstruction of first rate national importance. . . . The Trustees might initiate an educational advance which would be one of the greatest in the history of state education. They might make possible at last after a generation of discussion a really massive contribution to the rural problem which, it could be said without exaggeration, would surpass anything that had been done in any country (XVI).

This appeal to the Carnegie Trust, and numerous appeals to other sources of money, was to take up much of his energy until 1939. 'He was one of the more expert of beggars', wrote Leonard Elmhirst of the Dartington Trust (see p. 39). 'Unfortunately', Elmhirst went on, 'his period of major development courted considerable opposition in some quarters, and almost no interest from the University at his door.' It was in such a climate – where discouragement abounded – that Henry Morris set out on his journey towards his El Dorado: what is remarkable is that he arrived.[1]

1 Letter to the author.

THE CREATIVE ADMINISTRATOR

Morris's diplomatic tact and political skill have already been noted in connection with the Cambridgeshire Syllabus of Religious Teaching. His *Memorandum* on the village college, quoted in the previous chapter, gave evidence of his exceptional vision combined with a rare grasp of practicalities. But diplomatic and political victories were not enough, nor was it enough to dream dreams and sketch the outlines of future experiments. The experiments had to be made to work, and this demanded courage, energy and a readiness to risk independent action. Until that time these were qualities which committees of local authorities did not expect to find in their servants, few of whom had ever shown signs of possessing them in the past.

This independence was strikingly shown in Morris's persistence in raising private money for his public schemes. What Chief Education Officer today, on seeing his plans threatened by an uncomprehending and parsimonious committee, would have the cheek to take off for America and come back with a cheque so fat that no councillor could oppose his plans? And indeed this example which Morris provided of an administrator of independent thought and action was almost as important as the results he achieved in Cambridgeshire. After his first bold steps it was easier for an education officer to take an independent line as long as he knew, as Morris almost always did, how to 'carry his committee with him'.

His fund raising was not of course his only excursion into independence. He was always ready to launch into print, and later to broadcast, in order to disseminate his ideas among a wider public. As we shall see, he became outspoken about the necessity for making wise use of the mass media, as when in 1940 he urged his fellow education officers to come together and promote a Penguin Special, in order, as he said, to 'create' a public opinion favourable to educational reform after the war.

He came across well on the air and it is typical that it was in a radio talk in November 1946 [16] that he sketched out his philosophy of administration:

The characteristic of our time, and the mark of a technological civilisation, is the disproportionate growth of administration in relation to quality, and indeed as an end in itself. . . . I'm afraid that this baneful development is very evident in public education. More and more control of our education tends to be administrative rather than cultural. . . . The view I want to put to you is that administration is only safe when it is in the hands of the philosopher and thinker, the teacher and the artist and the saint for whom administration exists merely as the instrument for realising quality and value. Such people are always economical of their use of administration; for them three parts of quality goes with one part of administration. In our contemporary world it often happens that we have three parts of administration to one of quality.

Twenty years earlier he was emphasising the need for administration to be unobtrusive. On an endpaper of his own copy[1] of G. D. H. Cole's *Social Theory* he wrote: 'Good organisation seems in many cases to exist in inverse ratio to the excellence and quality of life. . . . Organisation should be noiseless, a means, a convenience, subsidiary and not dominant.'

The administrative style which emerged from this philosophy, although it could be claimed to have been successful in Cambridgeshire, did not in his day always work to his advantage. On the wider national scene, and in particular at the Board of Education, it earned him hostility. On some occasions his readiness and ability to proclaim his enthusiasms grated on the official mind. Sir Graham Savage, who was Chief Education Officer of the LCC from 1940 to 1951, has written significantly about him: 'As a colleague in the Association of Education Officers, he was occasionally amusing, for he could be provokingly witty, but for the most part he was maddening.'

There was, of course, no hint of this quality in the confidential references which Morris provided for the appointing committee of the Cambridgeshire County Council when he applied for the post of Assistant Secretary for Education in December 1920. All his referees agreed that he was exceptional:

'He possesses insight and vision as well as the faculty for dealing with concrete problems' (Salter Davies, Director of Education for Kent). 'He was one of the most thoughtful students I have ever had . . . his training involved in the Study of Moral Sciences bears directly on the problems facing the educationist' (W. E. Johnson, Fellow and Tutor of King's College). 'He is a man of decided ability and great independence of thought and character . . . who may be trusted to turn himself with abundant zeal and conscientiousness to whatever work he undertakes' (Hastings Rashdall, Dean of Carlisle, Fellow of New College, Oxford). 'Mr Morris is an unusual type. He possesses the spirit of the missionary combined with a keen practical sense . . . an enthusiast without being a dreamer. The administrative side of education needs men like him . . . who can view educational problems in their relation to other social and political problems' (Arthur

---

1 Books from his library were made available to friends after his death. This copy was bought by Ian Phillips, who pointed out the notes to me.

Richmond, Assistant Director, Kent Education Committee; formerly Private Secretary to Sir Robert Morant).

The appointing committee had been well served by these referees. None, however, had mentioned the fact, unless it was hidden in Richmond's phrase 'the spirit of a missionary', that he was supercharged with emotion, which in his early days at least he was not always able to control. His new chief, Austin Keen, cannot have found him an easy assistant. It was said by some that his first achievement in Cambridgeshire was to drive Keen to his grave. Certainly Morris found him 'insufferable, ignorant and intolerable', according to a letter he wrote to a friend in August 1921. He succeeded Keen in 1922.

Austin Keen was not the only one to find Morris hard to work with. Norman Fisher who started his career in educational administration under Morris in 1938 has written:

Given the limitations of staff in a small Education Office, an erratic chief of genius who was also a perfectionist, and one had an explosive situation. His staff could be divided into two parts. Those who could not cope with Henry at all, and those, while aware of his shortcomings, who remained entirely devoted to him. I belonged to the latter group [34].

Many of those who had never worked with him, including other education officers, used to suggest that he was not a successful administrator; he was, they suggested, too bohemian to be efficient. Fisher denied this totally, and from close experience: 'Only those who have worked with him can appreciate the minute and thorough devotion to detail, the intense concentration which he can bring to any administrative problem however humdrum' [33].

Fisher was one of a long line of 'apprentices' whom Morris took on at Shire Hall. The first of this line was Russell Scott, who was his first administrative assistant; later he became Headmaster of Cranbrook. Scott was a student at St John's, Cambridge in 1920 when he met Morris in the rooms of a mutual friend, Keith Innes. Morris had just started his 'learnership' in the Kent Education Offices. A common interest in music and in education brought them together. Scott played the violin and Morris accompanied him on the piano: 'He said it recreated us both . . . Henry was enraptured by Mozart . . . his technique was far from perfect, but his sensitive understanding of the Mozart idiom made his performance a joy to share.'

When Morris became Assistant Education Officer in Cambridge, he persuaded Scott to fill the vacancy he had left at Maidstone, as one of Salter Davies's learners. In 1922 Scott too was back in Cambridge having been invited by Morris once more to fill the position he had vacated, this time as Assistant Secretary of Education. Scott has written:

The Education Office was therefore staffed by a Secretary of 34 and an Assistant Secretary of 24, with $4\frac{1}{2}$ and $1\frac{1}{2}$ years experience respectively. At that time the County Council consisted of a high proportion of farmer backwoodsmen, vehemently opposed to any expansion of the education service, particularly if it entailed additional expenditure. They were ready to pick on the slightest excuse for criticising the Education Secretary's proposals, or for casting doubt on his efficiency. In consequence Henry became extremely touchy about mistakes in the office, and his nervousness was accentuated whenever the education committee's minutes were coming up for confirmation by the Council. He was meticulous about the composition of minutes, reports and letters. All administrative and educational jargon was to be avoided, while anything which showed some sign of conciseness and literary style received commendation: 'You must use athletic English', he would say. In the office, his high degree of nervous energy and his rhetorical style of speech induced in the staff an exceptional lift of the heart, or, if critical, plunged them into depths of depression. He could, and did, go into a tantrum over small errors in the office – delay in submitting a draft, filing a document in the wrong place, failure to bring some minor item of information to a school managers' meeting. Excuses were not tolerated, and if persisted in he would throw a pot of ink or a bottle of glue at the head of the unfortunate clerk. On one occasion he broke his fountain pen in two and threw it at the wall . . . nevertheless he was not a bully in the ordinary sense, for he would attack others in positions stronger than his own with as much ferocity as he would any subordinate.

Although there were days when Henry would come to the office looking thunder and freezing everyone into incompetence, there were others when things had been going well, and when his charm and enthusiasm were uppermost . . . then the office would hum. . . . These occasions became more frequent as his successes and confidence increased. He ceased to slavedrive, and in a fervour of enthusiasm would urge the staff on to greater efforts with: 'Forth beste out of thy stall.' 'The rapture of the forward view.' 'He who having put his hand to the plough . . .' Outright praise was by no means unknown.

David Hardman had a unique opportunity of observing Morris in action in committee. He was Assistant Secretary in the extramural department of the university, and a close friend of Morris's. He was a county councillor, a member of the education committee, and later became its chairman.[1] He remembers Morris as

always decorous and strict on protocol, and he of course knew more about the matter in hand than any of us. He showed little patience, however. When remarks or queries were made which to him were irrelevant or foolish, he would look across at me with undisguised contempt on his face. Or when I was in the Chair, would whisper: 'damned fool' 'doesn't know what he's talking about' 'drivel' 'idiot' etc. etc.

His eccentricities were a byword in the office. One of his assistants remembers him stopping in the middle of an important discussion and asking to be driven back to his flat as a matter of urgency. (He never drove a car.) When they arrived, he told his assistant to pour himself a

---

1 In the 1945 election he became M.P. for Darlington and was Parliamentary Secretary to the Ministry of Education 1945–51.

drink, and he disappeared upstairs. When he returned he was calm and relaxed: 'D'you know,' he said, 'I suddenly remembered I had forgotten to put on a vest this morning.'

As for the teachers in the county, although there were many who misunderstood his mission and his seeming aloofness, he early won them over in the most practical way. His reorganisation plans made it possible for him to persuade the County Council that a saving could be made in the number of teachers employed (several one and two teacher schools would disappear), retirements would not involve replacements, and there would thus be more money to increase the salaries of those remaining. As a result Cambridgeshire was able to adopt a policy of paying all its teachers on the new Burnham scale – an 'extravagance' which previously the county had refused to indulge in. This may partly have explained 'the prolonged applause' which greeted him when he addressed a meeting of the National Union of Teachers in Cambridge early in 1924, to introduce the very recently issued document: The Cambridgeshire Syllabus of Religious Teaching for Schools. He must also have received support from the NUT for his firm advocacy of 'training classes for teachers with distinguished lecturers', which had been one of the main recommendations of the report.

If his championship of the teachers brought them solidly behind him, 'and did much to soften their attitude to the somewhat dictatorial and high-handed new broom' (Scott) he was also able to win them over, in individual cases, simply through charm. Mrs Janet Jackson who had been head in four Cambridgeshire schools, has given a teacher's view, in a letter written in February 1970.

When he came to Cambridgeshire as Assistant, Mr Morris was then young and handsome and always charming. . . . He was sensitive to atmosphere, and on one occasion when I complained about my difficulties he said: 'But look at the children and their happy faces, you *have* your reward!' Although he knew so well what he wanted for children, he was always nervous and shy with them, and could not bear to be involved in any conversation with even the smallest groups. . . . I always found him most courteous and (if such a word is still permissible) 'gentlemanly'. . . . Whenever one went to his office for any sort of interview he would at the end of the visit, politely open the door and see one out. On one occasion I had rather a serious illness and, despite his many activities, he found time to write me a most kind and considerate letter.

His preparatory campaign, begun in 1923, had culminated in the religious concordat and the adoption of the Cambridgeshire Religious Syllabus. Following this the churches had allowed their schools to be truncated or closed, thus permitting the establishment of viable county schools for senior pupils. The first administrative obstacle to the village college plan, religious intolerance, had been removed. He quickly followed up this success. His committee, having received the first edition of his *Memorandum* in the last weeks of 1924, passed a motion in February 1925, unanimously approving the plan and setting up a special subcommittee to draw up a formal scheme for the consideration of the County Council, the Carnegie Trustees and the Development Commissioners. In the course of the council debate the Chairman, Councillor Hurrell, supported the scheme because he believed that it would

tend to keep the boys and girls of the villages in the country, instead of sending them into the towns. . . . The committee wanted some of their best boys left in the country to help with the farming. . . . As regarded (*sic*) the cost of the building of such a college they hoped the Carnegie Trustees and the Development Commissioners would bear a very large part.

At the same meeting Councillor Alfred Fordham, of Melbourn (who later was to become Chairman of the Education Committee) said he had read the report twice, 'and felt more and more that it was one of the most remarkable pieces of work that had been done for a long time'. Fordham's faith in the village college idea lasted for another thirty-five years, until his death.

It is interesting to recall an untidily scribbled note Morris wrote to a friend at the end of 1959 when he was already seriously ill: 'D. Eccles, the Minister, opens the Village College at MELBOURN on Friday, 11th December. This is Alfred Fordham's College. He is now dead. I am going. I wish to honour him. Am giving several pictures in memory. He backed the Village College policy from the first MOMENT in 1924 . . .' In this state of serious ill health, he still acted creatively, as well as loyally.

'EXPERT BEGGAR'

But even Alfred Fordham's support could not speed up the processes of Cambridgeshire local government, and it was not until October 1927 that the committee approved the scheme for the building of the first village college at Sawston; and approval was won only because members were told that the building of the college would cost them little more than the repairs and improvements necessary to bring the existing elementary school up to standard. Economies were being effected partly by grouping schools (thus reducing the number of teachers employed by the authority) but to a large extent because Morris had striven untiringly not only to raise money from Trusts and from individuals, but also to encourage firms and commercial or educational institutions to make gifts in kind to the new college, or to provide services and install them free. Thus the Bedfordshire, Huntingdonshire and Cambridgeshire Electricity Company had offered to give and install all the lighting and electric fittings without charge. Newnham College was to give their old laboratory benches. The Cambridge University Press offered a hundred pounds worth of books. A handsome fountain in the forecourt was paid for by Mr and

Mrs Griffith, artists who lived in Sawston, and £1000 was given by the Elmhirsts of Dartington to furnish a metal workshop. Several local notables gave sums of fifty or a hundred pounds. The Carnegie Trustees were the main donors; they gave £5400 plus a further £100 towards the fee of a consultant architect. Most important, the land on which the college was to be built was given by Messrs Spicers, proprietors of a paper mill at Sawston. Little encouragement came from the Board of Education.

The whole long-drawn-out operation which culminated in his committee's approval for Sawston had demanded continuous exertion, writing and amending memoranda, checking architects' plans, steering items through committee. And it was made the more taxing because of the overriding need for incessant begging. He hated this. In 1932 he was writing to a friend: 'All our schemes are held up until we can raise £30,000. I am on the track of an old man of 94 who has just decided to devote his fortune of a quarter of a million to social ventures. It is not exactly pleasant work, this chasing rich people.'

It was a task from which he was never to be freed, right up to his last illness. His gift for importunity is well illustrated in the correspondence he had, over the years, with Leonard Elmhirst, for whom he was one of 'the more expert of beggars'. And he should have known, for if Morris was an expert beggar, the Elmhirsts were almost legendary dispensers of enlightened charity throughout the second quarter of this century. Leonard Elmhirst had married an American heiress, Mrs Whitney Straight, in 1925. Progressive education and rural reconstruction were among their major interests. In 1925 they had bought Dartington Hall, in Devon, and founded there a community, which included a nursery school involving parents, and the now famous co-educational school. Here rural industries, forestry and progressive education were to be fostered. Morris no doubt felt that such interests would match his own, and in June 1928 he wrote to sound out Leonard Elmhirst. The response was cautious, but not unfriendly. Morris wrote again, enclosing a copy of *The Village College*, and other papers.

I cannot resist [he wrote] sending you other documents in order to illustrate our attempt to organise every possible part of local government in developing the social welfare of our rural area. On page 21 of my pamphlet you will see what we are after. Everything is ready except the buildings. Six synthesising buildings in six centres would do the trick; and one is certain. Then I think the whole rural problem in England would take on a new constructive phase. It is an immense chance – one can hardly sleep at night for thinking of it. And I do not know of such another ripe set of circumstances either in this country or elsewhere.

In the autumn of 1928 he went to Dartington, but no funds came as a result of the visit. In January 1929 he turned to Elmhirst again, referring to the possibility of the Rockefeller Foundation contributing £90,000 towards a grand scheme for a chain of village colleges in Cambridgeshire. In order to secure the gift he had to find three donors who would give £5000 each. He wrote:

I am taking my courage in my hands to ask you to come to our help by guaranteeing one sum of £5,000. It is a magnificent opportunity, after generations of discussion, to make a really crucial contribution to the rural problem which would be a model not only in this country but abroad. You know the rural problem, you do not require to be converted. Hence I come to you first . . . you could make possible the first step to success.

Leonard Elmhirst's reply was gracious but negative. However, in November of the same year (1929) Morris was begging from him again, explaining that he had just returned from America with an offer of £45,000 from the Spelman Fund, but in addition he needed £5000 to secure the backing of the county council for his scheme for six colleges.

After two years of negotiation we are in sight of success and it is difficult to contemplate failure at the last lap. I should tell you that we are preparing to have a nursery school included in each village college and to make it a centre not only for purely nursery school purposes but for the education of older girls and for parents.[1] We shall therefore realise some of the objectives of the Merrill Palmer School.[2] . . . I hope therefore that we in Cambridge will make some contribution to parental education and that you will be able to compare our work in this direction. You will forgive me I trust for writing to you again and in venturing to ask your aid.

This time the reply was procrastinating but not a total negative. Morris responded gratefully and on 2 December received his reward: 'Mrs Elmhirst and I are prepared to make four annual payments of £250 making in all a grant of £1000.'

In November 1930 he was writing again to Elmhirst. This letter reveals a number of facts. First the very small sums he felt he had to beg for. Secondly the attitude of benevolent paternalism (reminiscent of Lord Reith then at the BBC), which he adopted towards commercial entertainment. Thirdly his view of the Sawston cinema storm, which is touched on in the next section. And fourthly, his enthusiasm for Sawston in action.

Dear Elmhirst,
I am in a great difficulty, and am venturing to write to you for your help even though I realise that in doing so I may receive a rebuff. But in my job,

1 It is interesting to see him advocating, in 1929 what is only in the seventies becoming accepted – the co-operation of parents, older children, and experts in the education of infants.
2 The Merrill Palmer school in Chicago was an experimental nursery school. Morris knew that Elmhirst was interested in this as he had appointed to run the nursery school at Dartington, a young English girl, Winifred Hartley, who had studied nursery education at the Merrill Palmer school.

especially in a County of this kind, there are so few people of understanding to whom one can turn.

You will remember that we have provided for the Hall (of Sawston Village College) a properly fitted up cinema chamber. But we have no cinema machine, and my keen ambition to show how the cinema might become an instrument of real education and culture is held up. For some years Sawston has had a cinema in a local chapel provided by a local magnate. But this has been run on commercial lines and shows have been of the usual trumpery and insipid type. The local magnate was prepared to put his cinema into our Hall but under such conditions, from which he refused to budge, that the County Council, backed by the Carnegie Trustees, turned the offer down as being entirely against the spirit of the village college scheme, and one calculated, in fact, to wreck it. He demanded to have the Hall every Thursday, Friday and Saturday of the year to show what films he liked, and to run shows on a commercial basis and with the usual atmosphere and accompaniments of a cinema palace.

What I, and many people, especially the intelligent working people of Sawston want, is a Sawston Cinema Society. The cinema would be used in school time for lessons on geography, nature study, travel etc. Once or twice a week an evening show would be given for all the nine villages served by the Village College. In addition to entertainment films, in which a high standard would be secured, there will be other films of a really interesting and fascinating character shown. . . . Such films are easily available from the Society of Cultural and Educational Films . . .

In the meantime there is no cinema in Sawston, the local magnate having closed his down. My fear is that if we do not act quickly some commercial travelling film exhibitor will appear and spoil our field. This is the moment to start our scheme if we can get someone to present us with a cinema machine. A quite useful machine can be got for about £100 . . . two machines would enable us to give shows technically adequate from the point of view of speed and lack of interruptions.

It is a fine chance to show how a rural community can organise its own entertainment on a cultural basis, and to show how the cinema can be redeemed. Would this not provide an example to other rural areas and indeed to the towns? I am a poor man, but if we can get the necessary machine equipment I will start off the maintenance fund of the Sawston Cinema Society with a subscription of £5.

The Senior School at the College is going well. All the children of the nine villages turn up daily without a hitch. The children cheer as they board their omnibuses in the early morning. Those who are unwell refuse to stay away, or cry if they are compelled to do so. For the children of nine villages, school has become an adventure. Every day you can see 150 children taking a midday meal of two courses for 2½d . . .

The adult side is also going strong. The library is open every evening from 7 till 9. An average of 50 readers and borrowers turn up nightly. The university extension course has 100 students including young men and women who cycle in from the surrounding villages.

He went on for a whole page, describing the activities of numerous voluntary societies in the college, and the various classes in woodwork, 'cottage cookery', dressmaking 'specialising in renovations of old clothing'.

The Hall is used for weekly dances, mostly held for local objects such as the Nursing Association, and for a school fund to provide spare slippers for the use of Senior School pupils for use in school. The Centre for Juvenile Employment and Unemployment Insurance for the whole of Sawston is housed in the village college so that the Warden and his staff are able to keep in touch with the unemployed boys and girls and get them to come to evening classes . . .

Elmhirst's reply was short and regretful. 'I wish I could do the thing you ask, but ours is no widow's cruse.' Morris again answered gratefully, and admitted that there was a new possibility that 'they might be presented with a cinema by one of the manufacturers'. For however much he inveighed against the cultural workings of the commercial world or against capitalists 'with faces like plates', he was always ready to use their money.

In March 1932 he was writing again to Elmhirst:

I am going to America and Montreal to do what I can to save our Village College scheme from extinction. . . . I do not know how our situation appeals to you. The opportunity seems to me silver-gilt. Think of the influence on rural England of a scheme such as ours going on obstinately and sanguinely in this contemporary chaos of false opinions. And all that stands in the way of this constructive stroke is the miserable sum of £20,000. I do not hesitate therefore to ask your aid and advice. The prospect is ten Sawstons. . . . In these times every instalment of constructive work put in hand, especially in Education, is a gesture on behalf of reason and faith in human affairs.

It might be thought strange that Morris the administrator spent so much of his time 'chasing rich people'. But the 1930s were terribly lean years. If he had not battled, nothing would have been done.

STORMS OVER SAWSTON

In October 1930, three years after the go-ahead had been given, the Prince of Wales opened the first village college in the world, 'setting the seal of royal approval upon an ambitious scheme of rural education which has attracted world wide attention. In it Cambridge once again leads the way' (*Cambridge Daily News*, 30 October 1930). The Prince's speech in fact was a classic string of platitudes and clichés, which must have moved Henry Morris to silent scorn. An old man, T. F. Teversham, writing from Sawston in February 1970, recalled the occasion vividly:

Edward VIII (*sic*) was to open the meeting. I had collected funds towards the £500 the village had to provide to get the money which had been offered by some American – but I didn't get a ticket – nor did Smith, headmaster of

Shelford school; so Smith and I crept in and stood at the back. I watched a parish councillor whom I had vainly approached for a contribution; he was a fen farmer and known to be tight with his money, but being a Parish Councillor he was in the front row. What a terrible show it was; the dreadful reading, not a speech, by Edward VIII.

In spite of the speeches and the platitudes, in spite of the usual catfight for places which always occurs when royalty appears for a local function, 30 October 1930 must have been a great day for Morris. The struggle had been harsh, but the labour and the wounds had not been in vain. On that day the building, the staff and the students were real and were there, at Sawston. The building itself was far from revolutionary. It was designed by H. H. Dunn, county architect, in consultation with James Shearer brought in by the Carnegie Trustees. The *Cambridge Chronicle* of 29 October had rightly said: 'There is a suggestion of the eighteenth century about the general design of the open court, and there is a "colonial" influence in the building as a whole.' This surely was an unconsciously perceptive remark by the reporter.

But whatever one may think of its conventional design Sawston was the first county school of its size to have a separate hall, the first to have an adult wing, specially built and furnished suitably and attractively for adults, the first to have a library for shared use by the school and by the community. The first where the Youth Employment Office was housed in the school, and a mechanics workshop was provided, specially biased towards agricultural engineering (the latter paid for by Mr and Mrs Elmhirst). There were playing fields for use by both village and school, a medical services room and a Warden's house. Many of these features are commonplace today. In 1930 they were revolutionary. They would never have been included without the generosity of individual or collective donors; a generosity evoked only by the repeated and grinding exertions of Henry Morris: '*I have given my blood for Sawston – not my sweat, my blood.*' That was how in later years he recalled the fight. But at the time there was no sign of loss of blood. After the second war, a newcomer to the office staff remarked that Mr Morris was a fine looking man, and an old hand had replied: 'You should have seen him in the old days. You should have seen him at the opening of Sawston.'

He retained a special feeling for Sawston as his firstborn. Always irritated by the way the environments he had carefully prepared could be misused, especially if the offenders were 'his' teachers, when this occurred at Sawston there was no sparing the offender. John Watts, who became Head of Les Quennevais, a community college in Jersey, and is now Warden of Countesthorpe College in Leicestershire, started his career teaching English at Sawston after the war:

We worked in awe and fear of him. He was unpredictable, hawk-like in his visitations and merciless in his wrath if his eye was offended. The word would go round: 'Henry's on his way out'. The fountain would be turned on and the bronze animals that stood sentinel at the ornamental front doors would be brushed and oiled.[1]

He once arrived unannounced on a summer evening when I was rehearsing a scene from *The Winter's Tale* on the fountain lawn. I felt rather proud of this; children staying on after school rehearsing, while in one corner of the lawn was the choir singing a special setting by Margaret Wander, the music teacher, of one of the songs. Surely the great man, suddenly appearing at the front of the lawn would take this in at a glance and commend it with warmth. Not a bit of it. What he saw was that Margaret, to conduct her choir, was standing on one of the four precious marble balls that stood one at each corner of the lawn. He flew into a passion and shouted at Margaret to get off. The singing faded and in horrified silence the children heard from him that those marble balls had been transported by him all the way from Italy. The choir adored Margaret and asked me fiercely who that horrid old man had been. It is sad to think that there are people in Cambridgeshire now who may only remember him as that, and indeed teachers who only saw that particular aspect of his care for what was created.

Watts himself knew better. Showing his special concern for the staffing of Sawston, Morris himself had interviewed him; and had worked on him that teacher's spell which he cast on so many he came across, whether as friends or simply quite casual acquaintances, throughout his life. Watts recalls:

I found the interview I had with Henry Morris, when I was a candidate for the Sawston job, markedly different from any I had experienced before. It was more an exchange of enthusiasms than an interview . . . with talk flowing around Italian architecture, Plato and Dover Wilson's account of his using *Macbeth* with Day Continuation classes. What impressed me then was not only the personal charm, but the enormous exploratory energy, the sort of vision that could encompass both the secondary modern classroom and the Teatro Olympico at Vicenza. My direct contact with him after my appointment was, not unexpectedly, minimal, but the effect of starting a career knowing that education could and should be something other than a drab routine, should be part of a civilising tradition, was powerful and lasting; it coloured my life's work.

When Watts was appointed to the Community College in Jersey, he remembered Morris:

When I was equipping the school and local opinion was voicing hostility through the press and political channels against my 'lavish expenditure' on musical instruments, wall-papers, easy chairs for students' common rooms and so on, I thought of Henry fighting, cajoling, squeezing money from where none seemed to exist, to make Sawston so radically different from the expected community centre. He put walnut panelling all round the adult common room while everyone else was still thinking in terms of

---

1 Actually they were wrought iron animals presented by the Buxton Trust, specially designed by James Shearer, the Carnegie consulting architect; they still stand there.

ex-service huts and trestle tables. He collected works of art with loving care, and placed them within view of the children, and of the teachers and local people who came together there. He saw the college as a place where works of original art could interact with the creative activities going on there. The college was an instrument of civilisation.

Sawston may have become an instrument of civilisation, but the controversy which raged around it in the early years was far from civilised. It might today seem too trivial to recall it, and certainly it went on too long for it to be worth documenting all its petty twists and turns. But the Sawston storm shows us much about Morris. It reveals the depth of hostility he engendered, the lengths to which his enemies would go in attacking him, and the slings and arrows he had to suffer at the hands of those he no doubt thought of as outrageous philistines. It shows also what a suspect operator he could appear to be, and what an obstinate defender he was, not of himself but of his village college and of the high cultural standards which he persuaded his committee to maintain there. Here, briefly, is the story:

In Sawston there lived a certain H. G. Spicer, a landowner and proprietor of the Sawston paper mills. Mr Spicer liked to organise film shows for the village in a disused chapel; towards the end of the 1920s he decided to build a hall for the purpose. When Henry Morris heard of this, he went to see Mr Spicer and persuaded him to do three things: first to abandon his plan for building a special hall, secondly to give a parcel of land to the county council for the building of a village college, and thirdly to donate a sum of money towards the college. Spicer understood that he would be able to use the hall of the college for his film shows.

At about the same time meetings were held in the village to encourage the collection of £500 towards the building of the college, which was a condition laid down by the Carnegie Trustees for their donation of more than £5000. Morris was on the platform at two of these meetings and was questioned from the floor as to whether the Spicer film shows would be shown in the hall of the village college. Later there was disagreement among those who were present as to whether he had or had not given an unconditional assurance that the pictures would be shown there.

A few months after the opening of the college, the Managers were informed by the Education Committee that the request to show films in the hall on the last three nights of each week was not approved. There followed a series of vituperative attacks, on Morris and on the Education Committee, in the correspondence columns of the *Cambridge Daily News*, and in the council chamber at Shire Hall. The protagonist in the anti-Morris camp was Commander Eyre Huddleston, Council member for Sawston and friend of Mr Spicer. At a meeting of the County Council, on 5 May 1931, he accused Morris of breaking the promise he had made at the public meetings in Sawston, and of suppressing requests for the use of the hall for showing films. The *Cambridge Daily News* reported Huddleston's speech:

So conscious was he of a lack of straightforward dealing in this matter, so convinced was he that the village's subscription was obtained by means of a misrepresentation, that he had there a cheque for £500 which he proposed handing to the chairman in the hope that he (the chairman) would sanction the return of their moneys to those of the subscribers who had been duped. He would sooner bear this financial loss himself than that his name should be associated in any financial connection with that disgusting affair.

The Chairman of the Education Committee, Councillor Fordham, defended his officer unreservedly and pleaded with Commander Huddleston to 'end this continual baiting of the education secretary, this writing to the newspapers, and let us have peace'.

But peace there was not to be. Spicer built his own hall for showing his pictures, and sited it beside the village college, obstructing the view of the college as one approaches from Cambridge. At the opening of 'Spicer's Theatre' in September 1932, Mr Spicer himself chose to bring up the controversy again, reverting to his understanding of the 'agreement' he had made with Henry Morris concerning the showing of films in the hall of the village college. And in the following January, nearly three years after Sawston had been built, Commander Huddleston continued to vent spleen. The occasion was the presentation to Mr and Mrs Spicer of an album of appreciation signed by a thousand inhabitants of Sawston.

For my part [he said], while I am your representative I probably cannot prevent cadging money and gifts from America or elsewhere in support of fancy schemes. I may not be able to prevent the giving and breaking of promises, but I can and will prevent the hushing up of any public scandal such as that attendant on the financing of the first village college.

Huddleston's attacks were not confined to the financing of the college; he queried the composition of the managing body of the college, suggesting that it was packed with free churchmen; he queried the walnut panelling of the Adult Room (which so pleased John Watts), because it had largely been paid for by a private donor who remained anonymous; and he queried the visit to the United States of the Education Secretary and its possible financial implications. This was not a reference to possible misuse of public funds, but to the possibility that Morris might return bearing gifts for 'fancy schemes'; for, as he assured the committee, 'the word "gifts" stinks in the nostrils of the district I represent'. Finally he proposed a motion in the council chamber, in November 1932, 'that a committee of enquiry be set up to investigate and report upon the representations alleged to have been made by the Education Secretary for the purpose of obtaining local support and donations for the building of Sawston Village College'. The motion was lost.

Spicer's Theatre still stands, marring the approach to the college, but it is no longer called Spicer's Theatre, and it no longer shows films. It was bought by the County Council after the war, and is used by the college as a Youth Centre.

The people mentioned in this story were by no means Morris's only enemies on the council. He seemed almost to relish the drama involved in the attacks on him, and he did little to appease his opponents. Councillors tend to be suspicious of absentee officers and Cambridgeshire ones were not exceptional. In 1947 he made a three-month tour of West Africa at the request of the Colonial Office. On his return an irate alderman asked him: 'Who does your work when you are away from the office so often?' 'Precisely the same people who do it when I am not away,' replied Morris.

Peace feelers were sometimes put forward, but not from him. A landowner who was also a councillor, after years of battle with Morris, decided to try and patch up the differences between them and had a long conciliatory chat with him after a meeting. Afterwards in the seclusion of his office Morris jocularly suggested to his assistant that that would be worth at least a brace of partridge, but when at the weekend, the councillor's chauffeur arrived on Morris's doorstep bearing a hare, he was told to take it back to the donor since he never ate hare.

Like Oscar Wilde he was fascinated by the picture which the gospels give of Jesus facing a hostile and uncomprehending world, and would refer to his long lasting disputes with pharisaical or philistine laymen often in biblical terms. 'By these stripes we are healed,' he would say, perhaps to console himself. Or, to make his point he would quote the words from the cross: 'Father forgive them, for they know not what they do.' But he would not be heard to say: 'It is finished', although there must surely have been times when he felt that way: he once confessed that after a meeting at the Board of Education, when he had been vainly seeking support for the village colleges, he was so depressed that he nearly threw himself in the Thames.[1] He once explained his persistence: 'Were it not for the irrepressibility of ideas,' he said 'I should give up.'

It is not surprising that in the late twenties, while Sawston was still being built, he was busy with his Grand Design: a chain of village colleges which would follow it. This meant prospecting for money, for he realised that whatever Huddleston might say, his committee would never have accepted the builder's tender for Sawston amounting to £16,000, if half that sum had not been given, in money or services or kind, from outside sources. If he was going to persuade the councillors to commit themselves even to another three or four colleges, he would have to prise open their fists with a golden lever.

---

1 This may have been the occasion in 1924 on which he had a particularly fruitless meeting with the Minister himself, Lord Eustace Percy, whom he labelled ever afterwards as Lord Useless Percy.

A begging letter reminding the Carnegie Trustees of their generosity to Sawston brought no immediate response. Realising that, like many other prospectors, he must look West, he took a brave and original decision. In the autumn of 1929 he booked himself a return passage to New York. He had secured an introduction to the Spelman Fund of America, an offshoot of the Rockefeller charitable empire. After his return with a promise of £45,000 the Cambridgeshire County Council voted £25 towards the cost of his fare. He had paid for his journey himself with the help of a very substantial loan from his brothers in Southport, which he never repaid . . .

5 EXCURSIONS – PUBLIC AND PRIVATE

AMERICAN EXTRACT

Although he was hospitably welcomed, and although both officially and financially he had a fruitful trip, Morris did not enjoy America. However, on the return voyage, he got to know a young Englishman, Charles Fenn, who was to remain for thirty years a constant, if intermittent, source of delight, and sometimes of fury. Fenn has described this meeting:

I first met him in November 1929. I was then twenty-two and Chief Steward of the Tourist Class on the *Aquitania*. Henry had been visiting the Spelman Fund people in connection with a handsome gift they were making to the Village College scheme. One evening on the deck we fell into conversation; the thing that impressed me was that here was one passenger who found shipboard life inexpressibly boring and couldn't wait to get off. Something was mentioned about why Henry had been to America, and amongst other things he disclosed that he had a cheque in his pocket for some large sum and that this was to be used for some very worthy cause, so that his sufferings in spending six days each way on the Atlantic might be said not to be in vain. Somehow this brought us round to the question of banking, but I was quite out of my depth. Henry said there was a book in the ship's library with a chapter that explained it, and he would get it for me. The following morning he handed me the book – *The Intelligent Woman's Guide to Capitalism and Socialism*, by a writer named Shaw, whom I had heard of but never read. Since I had to be polite to all passengers there was no escape, so I dutifully started to skim through the pages. To my enormous astonishment this chapter on the boring subject of banking at once seized my interest, so that I read the chapter without skipping and immediately went on to the next and through to the end. . . . That meeting and that book changed my life.

For Henry Morris the meeting was equally important, and the impression as lasting. But the friendship which began then was uneven – Morris's special feeling for Fenn was unrequited. In a letter to Fenn in March 1932 he made one of his frequent references to their first meeting; it was for him a kind of birthday, marking the passage of time, which always fascinated him.

The echo of the Aquitania reached me strangely. Do you realise it is now

two years and a half since I met you on the tourist promenade deck;
Terrible, this flow of Time.

> 'And at my back I always hear
> Time's winged chariot hurrying near . . .'

We have to seize life with all its potentialities, making a fresh start every
day, especially while the vitality, sensitiveness and pliability of youth are
with us.

Every day since his return from the American trip, Morris had
been making fresh efforts to forward his grand design. The cheque
from the Spelman Fund of New York was for £45,000 and, with a
promise of this sum literally in his pocket, he was able, on 1 April
1930, to present a highly attractive prospectus of the future village
colleges to his committee. The newspapers, reflecting the euphoria of
the council chamber, were ecstatic. Morris knew his committee,
and had remembered the bait which had landed Sawston; here is the
breakdown of the estimated funding of his scheme for ten more
village colleges, which he put before the members:

From the County Council	£37,481		£37,481
	———		
From Government Grant	£39,481	£39,481	
From the Spelman Fund, New York	£45,000		
From Mr & Mrs Elmhirst	£1,000		
From the Buxton Trust	£200		
From the Trigg Foundation (Melbourn)[1]	£858	£47,058	£86,539
	———		
			£124,020

He argued that the costs of maintenance and loan charges would be
covered by the savings effected on teachers' salaries arising from the
grouping of the schools involved in the scheme, and at the end of his
report urged the committee to set their sights boldly on the future:
'Time is on the side of a system of Education Centres; each succeeding
year will confirm its soundness, and inevitably the wise policy of
1930 will, by 1940 or 1950, have become the obvious one.'

The report, in the *Cambridge Daily News* of 2 April was headed:
'£45,000 Plum for Cambs'. It quotes the speech made by Alderman
Webber, chairman of the Finance Committee:

The figures are not only interesting, they are startling. The position is so
favourable that the county would be ill-advised to turn down the scheme
presented. The council have got hold of a real plum. If we do not carry out
this scheme in the near future, we shall have to carry out some scheme in

---

1 Councillor Fordham was a member of the Trigg Foundation Governing Body
and was surely influential in obtaining this sum. (See page 38.)

the distant future, and without the benefit of these gifts. The council will secure for a cost of £37,481 what, in ordinary circumstances, would cost £124,020.

The report in the Cambridge paper did not mention Morris by name, nor did the very full and understanding report which appeared in *The Times* of the following day; the style is not dissimilar from Morris's own, and this may account both for the omission of his name and for the understanding. Finally *The Times* on 4 April devoted a leading article to the village college idea, which exposed the wide significance of a scheme

which marks a step forward in the provision of advanced education in rural areas, and in other aspects promises to be an interesting experiment in the organisation of village life. . . . The feeling that there should be in every village a definite focus for its activities has grown strongly since the war, though sometimes the aspiration has taken rather vague forms. Strengthened however by the necessity for meeting the demands of education and other statutory services, it may well attain a new impetus. While there are regrettably disintegrating influences at work in rural England, there are also others, such as the modern power of locomotion, which, if rightly used, can be made to work for consolidation . . . and schools within manageable distances of some five or six adjacent villages are now much more than possibilities. And if there are to be schools and school buildings, why not, if the funds can be raised, enlarge them into something still more comprehensive, like the Sawston Village College and the others which are to complete the Cambridgeshire scheme?

Why not? Largely because the financial crisis of 1931 blocked all school building projects for the next three years. But even in 1934 when, at last, restrictions were lifted, and the Board of Education issued its first building regulations since 1914,[1] their attitude to the village college ideas was no warmer than when, in 1924 a civil servant had called it: 'this pretty bubble'. It is true, that the 1934 Regulations recommended that school buildings should be graceful, bright, colourful; the provision of a hall, a medical room, and a library was to be encouraged; but, almost as an afterthought, the village college was mentioned as an idea which would have to remain, for some time to come, attainable only through 'private munificence'; though it was admitted that 'there is no reason why the village school should not be developed on similar lines as far as possible'.

For anybody, in those lean and barren years of the early 1930s, the grinding work of educational administration was almost continuously depressing. For someone with Morris's creative urge it caused endless frustrations which could only be tolerated if he could match them with private delights, from which almost all the people with whom he was forced to work were, by their very nature, excluded. He wrote on

1 *Elementary School Buildings*, Education Pamphlet no. 107/1936.

2 March 1932 to Charles Fenn (who was then working with a textile firm in Philadelphia):

I have been living for two weeks in a world of administration, of regulations, of abstract curricula, of educational 'isms' dry as dust; indeed, dusty as death; of reports, resolutions and recommendations discussed ad nauseam by dried up old men and women with bald heads and spectacles and all withered from the armpits downwards; a valley indeed of dry bones in which there is no life, and no suspicion of beauty, truth and goodness. But above all no apprehension of light and delight, of impulse and passion; of Art at once sensuous and sensual; of the satisfaction of pure intelligence; of food and wine; of the imperious demands of the body; of love encounters, most vehement and prodigal; of erections, masturbation, and expressible desire profound enough to shake the cosmic order; of sexual congress in which all reality seems to be absorbed and ultimately quieted, with calm of mind, all passion spent; or sunlight on the English countryside; morning sun in cornfields; the moon on the river; chicken and salad and claret cup for supper; dozing conversation in the Library; love and reality and the utmost physical enterprise under deliciously stiff linen sheets.

He was writing again on 10 March 1932:

The news of your visit in July is most interesting. I shall expect you to stay in Cambridge for several days at least. My visit to the U.S.A. is still uncertain . . . but you may be sure that I shall let you know well in advance. It will be astonishingly good to meet a friend, especially an Englishman, in New York. I am much depressed by the political situation. . . . We seem to be living in an interim period when we know what ought to be done, and have not the will to apply the remedies principally because of private vested interests, and unenlightened capitalism and economic individualism. I suppose the U.S.A. is worse because of the universal desire to make money and the romance of moneymaking. All our schemes are held up until we can raise another £30,000. Looking forward to seeing you either in New York or here . . . and when you come here I shall give you a gala dinner – good food and wine: especially Hock.

They did meet, briefly, later in the year, when Morris paid a flying visit to the United States to look for further funds,[1] and to lecture, at the invitation of Professor Fred Clarke, in Toronto. But it was not until Roosevelt was President and the USA began to emerge from the slough of the depression, and when the New Deal heralded a more expansive and optimistic mood, that a third and less hurried trip to the States became possible. Relatively unknown in his own country, Morris's name and ideas were already known to American educationists and New Dealers, so that in December 1933 he received the following flattering telegram from the Secretary of the Spelman Fund, New York:

[1] See letter to Elmhirst, p. 32.

To Henry Morris, Cambridge.

FEDERAL AUTHORITIES EARNESTLY DESIRE YOUR COUNSEL ON COMMUNITY
PLANNING IN SUBSISTENCE HOMESTEAD PROJECTS UNDER TWENTY FIVE
MILLION DOLLAR PROGRAM NOW BEING DEVELOPED. COULD YOU VISIT THIS
COUNTRY FOR POSSIBLY TWO MONTHS BEGINNING EARLY JANUARY AT SPEL-
MAN FUND EXPENSE. SEASONS GREETINGS. MOFFETT.

Kingsley Martin of the *New Statesman* saw the significance of the
invitation and wrote in his London Diary on 27 January 1934:

Some ten years ago I made the acquaintance of Henry Morris and heard
him explain his bold and original scheme for providing country people with
an opportunity for educating themselves. Since then he has done in Cambridge exactly what he said he would do, the most tangible achievement
being the creation of the remarkable village 'college' at Sawston. He planned
and built the place out of his own head and in the face of persistent discouragement. It was a considerable achievement both imaginatively and
practically, and it promised important results as a model for the development of a distinctively rural English culture, on a community basis. His
schemes for improving and extending it in other zones were frustrated by
the crisis, aided by the opposition of local vested interests. But where his
own countrymen were hesitant a foreigner has pounced, and while the
educational lights of Cambridgeshire are still rubbing their eyes, and
wondering what to do with this strange fellow, President Roosevelt has
hauled him off to America, placing at his disposal a sum of 25,000,000
dollars to spend on rural community centres. Mr Morris has already sailed.
I gathered Mr Roosevelt thinks that the job should take him three months,
though I should not be surprised if he stayed there longer. I hope, at any
rate, that when the prophet returns to his own country he will not continue
to be without honour.

For Morris this invitation was not only an opportunity to be
associated with something big in the development of community
planning, it was a chance of again contacting Charles Fenn who was
still with the same firm in Philadelphia: a letter of 5 January 1934
announced his imminent arrival, and in another, scribbled on 16
January from the Hotel St Regis on 5th Avenue, New York, he
invited Fenn to stay with him in Washington: 'I will book you a
room, you will come please, as my guest. I am here to advise in the
carrying out of a community project costing 25 million dollars. . . .
It is an interesting experiment. . . . I sail back on the Savoia at the end
of the month to Italy to spend Easter there. Will you come?'
Fenn wrote of that visit:

On the whole Henry disliked America, because he was usually immured in
cities. . . . He found his American colleagues pedantic and verbose; he
referred to the 'triple distilled pontification of pallid academics' and on one
occasion, when some educationist made a long and platitudinous speech
about 'searching for the new education along empirically pragmatic lines'
he recalled with delight the honest admission 'Frankly, Doctor Morris, we
are all groping in the dark'. He was pressed to prolong his stay, but by

March could stand it no longer. Our times together were partly spent riding out into the countryside in my A Model Ford. This would do a top speed of 55 mph and, as the speed limit was strictly 40, we were on one occasion picked up by the New Jersey traffic police and hauled into court on the spot. The cop left to guard us was swinging his baton, and Henry opened up to this cop with a quip about the baton which, he said, would, a thousand years hence, adorn the shelves of some museum as a remarkable relic of the phallic fetishism of the twentieth century. The cop didn't take kindly to this persiflage; Henry was suddenly seized by the shoulder and threatened with the baton: I hurriedly made signs to the cop that Henry was mental, a suggestion he had no difficulty in accepting as true. . . . Henry never forgot the almost savage wrath of this cop, and it proved to be one of several incidents which alienated his original goodwill towards America.

Another time he came along with me to a party connected with a business convention. One of my associates was mayor of his local town and precentor of the Presbyterian church. Henry had a pleasant chat with this man, whose ancestors came from a part of England he knew well. . . . Along with drinks and food, a few highly paid whores were distributed for the convenience of the guests and subsequently Henry, wandering through the suites of rooms, looking for a drink, came across this mayor in a bedroom, tears in his eyes and without his trousers. He was lamenting that he had fallen a prey to one of these girls. 'What was troubling him,' Henry told me, 'was not the sinful nature of the deed, but the possibility of contracting clap. . . . Somehow I feel an English mayor and precentor would have given precedence to sin; these Americans never get their values right.' This was only partly flippant; he shied away from the sordid and said that this party plumbed the depths.

GREEN AND PLEASANT ENGLAND

Letters to Fenn, after Morris returned to Cambridge, contained sharp comments about America, often followed by enthusiastic outpourings about the English countryside, about further projects for village colleges, or plans for memorable holidays they would spend together. The first letter was written 12 May 1934:

Your letter came yesterday, as vigorous as ever, and very good reading. But first I must tell you how much I owed to you during my visit. You were a very present comfort in time of isolation and it was reinforcing to see you and talk. . . . It was good to be with you. . . . I wish women could share one's intellectual life more, and one's sense of humour and one's philosophic outlook. I left you at the harbour at New York with a pang . . . not a romantic one (of course) tho' I shed an inward tear but wondering when we should again renew our intellectual and artistic explorations. I want to send you books. . . .

England was a lyric when I arrived. Jack Pritchard met me on the boat and bore me off in a car to join an Easter weekend with his wife and three others on Dartmoor. Dartmoor was lovely – all green and gold with clear streams and fine skies and exquisitely trim villages and, further inland, immaculate country houses surrounded with flowers and deep, deep green lawns and daffodils.

I have been overwhelmed with work since I returned. This last week I have got off an appeal to the Carnegie Trustees for £10,000 towards the cost of three more Village Colleges, which are to cost in all £40,000. If I can get this job through I am thinking of deserting my job here and going to London to start a new educational weekly . . . one of the main objects would be to win teachers and the educational world over to Socialism and planning.

This is Sunday. I have been swimming and sunbathing and playing deck tennis in a lovely garden in the country . . . a typical English garden full of spring blossoms, lilac, hawthorn and tulips.

I must send you books . . . don't forget a wide range of reading – poetry, history, literature and the Arts . . . and music by the gramophone. I shall write again and shall look forward to a letter from you – your letters invigorate me. If I could talk I could go on for hours.

Dear U.S.A. – how distant it all seems; how prodigious and immense seems Europe and its culture by comparison, and Europe's leisure, and certitude and style.

> Ever yours,
> Henry.

P.S. Remember me to Miss Naval officer's daughter: she occasionally appears in my *dreams* and melts in my hands!

P.P.S. I am progressing in discarding dead bodies;[1] I wish I could go the whole hog. One ought to – and wine? One should? In any case one can give up flesh fairly easily, and be the better at least in having no responsibility for the (literally) bloody exploitations of lower animals. . . . Wine does not harm the grape . . . vegetarianism is a *moral* matter.

The haphazard juxtapositions in this letter, of seemingly unrelated subjects, appear confused; but there is a theme behind the confusion, directing the irregular flow and sequence of ideas: several times, after recalling the squalor of the States he contrasts it with the delights of the English countryside, or of English gardens, or simply of Cambridge.

He was writing again on 26 November 1934, recalling his American visit:

The summer has faded into winter. Christmas is here. It is almost a year since I set sail to the U.S.A. and having rung you up careered through Philadelphia and Maryland on that rather beautiful evening, robbing petrol pumps[2] (I mean gasoline stations) and reached Washington and supped at midnight in that restaurant . . . I mean cafeteria (groceteria, chemisteria, fishiteria, haberdashiteria, bookiteria, beeriteria, rubbergoodsiteria . . . and so on).

---

1 Fenn had recently taken up vegetarianism.
2 Fenn has explained that the filling stations were all closed so having run out of petrol they helped themselves to the dregs of petrol left in the feed pipes of every pump they passed.

Almost immediately following this catalogue he writes:

How is one to achieve the art of living and take part in the constructive reformulation of life's possibilities for the sake of those who come after? . . . This I find the daily problem as I get up, and see the beautiful English sky out of my bedroom window and walk through Cambridge's lovely gardens to my office.

In the same letter, he returned to his anti-American theme:

I have definitely come to the conclusion that America is not as important as I used to think some years ago. In the economic sphere I think she will carry out a gradualistic reform of the capitalist system on lines of English Liberalism. I doubt whether America will show much originality in economic reform, or policital invention. The former problem is already potentially solved. The race's real problem is cultural and religious – and here I think that America during your and my lifetimes will not do much. On the other hand I think England will probably show the way . . . she has such stores of maturity. . . . If I were 20 I would not any longer want to settle in America. I should still want to take a small share in the humane development of civilisation. . . . I spend Christmas very quietly with my sister[1] in the country and with her children. Likewise Easter when I shall walk for exercise. The summer must be prepared for; I feel we must make for the Yugoslavian coast. Meeting at Genoa. Across Northern Italy to Venice and Trieste, then a boat down the coast, stopping at various places until we reach Ragusa, where the bathing is specially arranged for archangels.

In December he made a decisive move. He wrote inviting Fenn to come and live in Cambridge at his flat. He had recognised Fenn's potential and the plan was for him to become, as it were, his apprentice, articled to him as the master. Fenn would in this way start to make a career in the English education system, perhaps in administration, perhaps in adult education.

The first necessity was to get a degree, and Cambridge was the place to get it. Fenn at first was dubious, yet deeply grateful and strongly tempted. Although he had quite a good job in a textile firm in the States he hated the commercial world in which he felt himself trapped. When he said he would come Morris showed his delight in a typical burst of words:

23rd January '35
I rejoice at your decision. A new prospect opens out for you. 'The world's great age begins anew . . .' Italy, land of beauty, and form and amenity. and Cambridge, and lovely England; all these you have in store; and Germany and Scandinavia, etc etc. And intellectual inquiry *and* freedom *and* *constructive work.*

1 This was his elder sister, Elizabeth Rimmer. Her husband was the principal of Wigan Technical College. They had a cottage at Bethesda, North Wales.

Cambridge:
Wed: 23 Jan: '35'

My dear Charles'
Your letter has just
been brought in as I go to London for
a two-days conference. I rejoice at
your decision. A new prospect
opens out — In fine,

The world's great age begins
anew....

I did not write again, wishing
to leave you free to decide.

, Italy, — land of beauty
and form and antiquity —
and Cambridge, and lovely
England: all these you have in
store: and far away, Scandinavian
circles: And intellectual
opening and freedom, and Constructive
work.

Part of letter Henry Morris wrote to Charles Fenn on 23rd January, 1935.
See page 56.

In the following months he continued in his letters to 'promote' England and Europe to the detriment of America. In March he wrote:

I shall send a note to be kept on the ship pending your coming on board. . . . I picture the horror of those slummy environs of the port which we taxied through together. Like you I felt the fundamental ugliness of America, and its incurability. I was staggered by the lack of felicity in the countryside. I never found a beautiful spot. And in the South . . . indeed everywhere . . . I noted, with misery, the all-pervading subtle unconsecrated lacerating ugliness and squalor. The black trash and the white trash, and the shacks and the debris and the advertisements, and the cruel inhuman, unsanctified ugliness. And the endless talk, and noise . . . no contemplation or beauty there. America is purely economic; blindly, competitively economic, devoid of the values of true civilisation.

Last weekend I walked near here and thought of Herrick's lines to the Daisy . . . which is blooming in profusion at this time of the year, and (as you know) closes up long before sundown:

> 'Shut not so soon
> The dull eyed night
> Has not as yet begun
> To lay a seizure on the night
> Or to seal up the sun
> No marigolds yet closed are
> No shadows great appear
> Nor doth the early shepherd's star
> Shine like a spangle here . . .'

Three weeks later he was writing again:

Five weeks on Saturday you ought to be dining here in my flat. I hope we shall fairly murder a bottle of Hock:

> 'The world's great age begins anew
> The golden years return
> The earth doth like a snake renew
> Her winter weeds outworn
> Heaven smiles and faiths and empires gleam
> Like wrecks of a dissolving dream.'

This is to point your thoughts as you pass from the beggared new world to the distracted old world of Europe . . . I hope the bathing will be warm enough when you arrive . . . it ought to be. The bathing place is delicious . . . it looks across a fine stretch of English pasture and woodland and towards Granchester. . . . Think of the silly old cocktail parties in the Aquitania, and the bored drivelling 'merriment' of everybody!

The next letter, less than a week later, returns to his American theme:

The Americans would prefer Wagner and Brahms to Mozart – but the American taste in the Arts is always wrong. Mozart is of course the greater artist, as everyone in Europe would agree without argument. America will discover that as they grow more mature and develop a real culture. But at present they are a commercial nation obsessed by the instruments of life, and by the economic process as an end in itself. America has not yet achieved a civilisation in the sense that European nations have and as e.g. Greece did . . .

The spring is beginning in all its glory. . . . I was overwhelmed by it when I got off the boat at Southampton; and so will you be.

So much for the reactions of Morris to America, comparable to those of many an intellectual Englishman, from Dickens onward, and not altogether surprising, seeing that Morris had deliberately left and abandoned his native south Lancashire – with its own ugliness and materialistic outlook – for the green fields of Grantchester and the civilised elegance of Cambridge. Possibly also there was another reason why his outpourings against America should be so regularly accompanied by praise of Britain and Europe; the point is made most clearly when Morris says: 'If I were 20, I should not want to settle in America.' Fenn was then in his middle twenties. In these letters, Fenn is being invited to see the American wasteland through Morris's eyes, and to compare it with the green and pleasant and highly civilised Cambridge, England and Europe, and make his choice.

HIS PROBLEM

Morris once drew the attention of George Edwards, his assistant, to a quotation from Archbishop Lang's autobiography: 'My life is rather a lonely one, it needs not friends, I have plenty of them; not work, I have too much of that; but just that simple human thing: someone in daily nearness to love.' This was a sad confession for an Archbishop to make. That Morris obviously felt he could apply it to himself is poignant. He very seldom asked for pity. But in a letter to Fenn in October 1936 he came near to it:

I find myself a problem, even amid engrossing work. There is this damned eternal sex problem. What can one do? One needs in spite of a host of friends, a centre of private affection, mental, spiritual, and physical. The usual solution is closed for me. Tell me what you think. Remember how-ever that I am never defeatist, and have enough resilience and philosophy to persevere under the most difficult disabilities. But the ideal I have mentioned mocks one, and is most dearly desirable; and it would make life doubly fruitful.

Morris's homosexuality cannot be overlooked. It explains some of his virtues and some of his eccentricities. Malcolm Ross, who was Warden of Sawston until he became Head of the big ILEA compre-hensive school, Crown Woods, has suggested that:

sexual frustration underlay a good many of the tantrums and brainstorms for which he was notorious. . . . It also helps to explain perhaps the precise nature of some of his priorities . . . his obsessive regard for neatness and what one might call the housekeeping aspects of the village colleges. Irritating as it was to have a man visiting you weekly who evaluated your job in terms of the number of dandelions you had permitted the gardener to overlook in the lawn in front of the fountain court, it was at the same time an assertion of neglected values.

Morris hid his shyness in the presence of women by displaying a charm which almost always precluded friendship. In a letter quoted on p. 54, he regretted the seeming impossibility for women to share in a man's intellectual or philosophical world. He made exceptions. Jacquetta Hawkes was a genuine friend, and Nan Youngman, whom he appointed as art adviser to the county at the end of the war, was someone whose intellect, taste and opinions he genuinely admired. There were others, but few. He also had a real interest in women as child bearers. David Hardman remembers him sitting next to his wife on the sofa in their house, turning to her and saying: 'Barbara, at the present moment, you are at the height of the biological urge.' Several women have recalled how he openly urged them to get together with their men and reproduce. Margaret Hinton, sister of Professor Colin Clarke, when she was teaching at a Cambridgeshire village school remembers him as 'a great believer in marriage for others. He openly encouraged Howard in pursuit and was our best man.'

A homosexual faces problems even today; in the first half of the twentieth century, and especially for a man in public office, these problems were almost insuperable. He almost overcame them, to a large extent through a conscious effort at sublimation. He would, in fact, often and openly say: 'We must sublimate or perish.' He was therefore driven to concentrate almost to excess on his work, and on the pursuit of beauty in the arts. When in 1959 he took, for some months, a house at Hurstpierpoint, he used often to visit David Hardman who lived nearby. Hardman's young children used to call him: 'That beauty man', because of his habit, when they were out walking together on the Downs, of suddenly stopping, extending his arms, and exlaiming: 'Beauty, beauty, how could we live without beauty?'

He strove to keep his emotions, as well as his mind, fully employed. In a programme for a Teachers' Course at Impington he arranged once for a significant quotation from Charles Darwin's autobiography to be prominently featured:

If I had to live my life again I would have made a rule to read some poetry and listen to some music at least once every week; for perhaps the parts of my brain now atrophied could thus have been kept active through use. The loss of these tastes is a loss of happiness, and may possibly be injurious to intellect, and more probably to moral character, by enfeebling the emotional part of our nature.

But sublimation was not a total solution. In another letter to Fenn, written in November 1936 he wrote:

In this sex matter one has to beware of becoming too dependent on one person. . . . For me it is more difficult than for you. I find myself developing intense likings and they are maddening. Then they come to an end, after much waste of emotion and wear and tear. I can stand the expense of extremely imperative and exciting and attractive physical experiences and I should be sorry not to have them. It is the love affair that is intolerable. I am just emerging from one.

Throughout his life he seems to have been seriously and deeply in love with only a small number of people. Although Fenn was entirely heterosexual, he felt a genuine sympathy for Morris, and he did not hide this. Morris therefore wrote openly to him about what he referred to as his 'problem', and on occasions discussed it with him.

He once admitted to Fenn his regrets at not being able to envisage marriage for himself. He would have welcomed the lasting and close companionship this would bring, and the experience of fathering and bringing up a family of his own. He was not at ease in the company of women; he was actively embarrassed by patently homosexual men, for his style, his outlook and his inclinations were the antithesis of the pansy or the camp. For this reason, many people, even among his friends, were unaware of his homosexuality.

Fenn has observed that, in fact, his emotional needs were often well served by an assurance of affectionate regard and admiration, and no more. Of their relationship, he has written:

His inversion was for me a cloud that would occasionally come across our sky. I had to accept the reality of this cloud as one might accept, in a close friend, the cloud of dipsomania or a neurosis. But Henry's personality was joyous and vivacious. His awareness of the arts, of nature, of the human episode, of life in all its manifestations was transmuted by Henry into an electric vibration that impinged on all his friends. My own admiration and gratitude for what he gave included genuine affection, understanding and acceptance.

His admiration for me was partly in response to this, and partly because I faced life without taking refuge in sentimentality. In addition I was a completely willing pupil who learned from him continuously. . . . He accepted my heterosexuality, and once said that he drew as much pleasure from this as from his own homosexual relationships. He certainly got enormous vicarious pleasure from associating himself with a man he loved, yet who actively loved women. He was not the first homosexual to feel this way:

> 'But since he pricked thee out for women's pleasure
> Mine be thy love, and thy love's use their treasure.'

AN UNEVEN FRIENDSHIP

During the early months of 1935 Morris continued to plan for Fenn's stay in Cambridge. In February he entered him for St John's College. In order to matriculate Fenn needed only to take a Latin examination; Morris advised coaching. Time was short. Fenn was to sail at the end of April on the *Aquitania*, where they had first met. Morris wrote on 4 April:

> I should love to be with you on the dear Aquitania.
> I think of her always with affection . . .

I am glad to think that you will be arriving in Cambridge when she is at her best and most entrancing. And how you will love the surrounding countryside – the river and the pubs hidden in villages where one can sit after a swim and talk. I hope you will have lots of books to read on your way over, including much poetry. This is the home of Milton, Dryden, Gray, Byron, Wordsworth (St John's), Coleridge, Tennyson.

Fenn arrived in Cambridge early in May. The dream became reality for a few months; then as we shall see, reality shattered it, and with it, for a time, their friendship. But the bonds of affection were not really broken, and grew strong again after Fenn returned to America. This may be explained by the unsentimental, the unromantic quality of the bonds upon which Morris always insisted, and which suited Fenn. In one of his letters (quoted below) anticipating Fenn's arrival in Cambridge, Morris referred to this absence of romanticism as being 'a rock'. And yet he had begun the same letter (5 March 1935) with an admission, indicating the kind of impatient concern every separated lover has always felt for the postman's arrival.

I have found myself in the past months looking for the long white envelopes with the American stamp and the unmistakable writing . . . and looking up the arrivals of the mails in *The Times*.[1] How barren have the times in between the arrival of letters seemed to me.

You say how glad you will be to set foot here in your home, meaning my home – but it will be our home, yours as much as mine. . . . I read your description of 'C. Deck Aft' with profound interest.[2] What a fateful meeting. I remember I felt shy. And that I found your warmth and energy reassuring. . . . The walk on the deck remains fixed in my visual memory indelibly.

I long like you for the Italian trip. I think we shall be able to take a perfect holiday such as I have never had, tho' I have had many holidays with good and wonderful friends. But we shall be able to do it perfect justice . . . finding a union of interest in all kinds of manifestations of life, and at the same time greedy of interest in architecture, in the scenery, in the people . . . and oh the sun and the landscape and the beauty. The one rock in this business of course is the absence of romanticism, and the sharing of intellectual, political, aesthetic and philosophic interests (as deep as passions and as real as food).

Fenn writes of his Cambridge experience:

When he wrote to me about going to the university, I had many misgivings. I hated the idea of sponging on him for three years. There were no

---

1 The movements of passenger lines were daily reported in the press.
2 This was a short story of two strangers meeting on a transatlantic liner, which Fenn had sent to Morris.

student grants in those days and Open Scholarships were for the very few. In accepting his invitation I took him at face value. It never struck me that he didn't mean what he said. He of course thought he meant it. . . . I weighed the odds and thought I should accept, since getting out of the rat-race meant so much to me. I had to pay two fares across the Atlantic – my own and my father's. During the six months I was in England, and including a holiday abroad, Henry provided bed and board but nothing else and finally the funds I had were quite exhausted. When I knew that in spite of his affirmations a sexual relationship was not excluded, there was nothing for it but to return to America. I had, of course, been absurdly naive. When I had to borrow the return fare from Henry he flew into a rage and we parted enemies; later when I sent him the first bit of repayment he at once became his old delightful self; and it can be seen from his later letters that he was never so admiring and affectionate a friend as during the subsequent years.

The letters of later years do indeed bear this out. One of them, written a year after the break on 5 October 1936, begins:

It was a real pleasure to get your brief note. . . . I think of you regularly; inevitably, in view of the times we have had together and the many momentous meetings in the U.S.A. and here . . . I regret always that you are not living in England so that one could have the most successful of all relations . . . independence with regular meetings.

Another letter ends with a vibrant postscript:

Heavens, there is no one in all England or Europe or America whom this week I would so eagerly be with or talk with. I have just finished a batch of memoranda and have heard a Beethoven and a Brahms quartet. The scene here is lovely and I have walked before dinner through King's gardens which you know so well, with thousands of daffodils in full bloom. Such beauty. But I think of all the political discussions we might have and the philosophical discussion and the laughter, and the intellectual agreement devoid of romance and illusion. And the swim tomorrow! Beer and sandwiches at Grantchester! Somehow, somehow we must meet again with abysmal satisfaction such as seldom occurs amongst humans. I salute you most real of spiritual companions I have known: the person I have most liked and trusted of all.

The following March (1937) he writes:

Dearest Charles, Your shaft of verbal light came two days ago. I go to Italy on Wednesday for 10 days most necessary sunshine. . . . We shall probably indulge the spirit and the imagination without which all flesh is as dust, but we shall value the food and the chianti. I could wish nothing better than that you were with me.[1] Are you reading? You must, systematically.

1 I was with Morris on this holiday. (See p. 94.) I had no idea Fenn existed! It was rather an unsuccessful trip – the necessary sun failed to appear at all, and Florence was wet! *H.A.R.*

I must send you some books. Here's beauty to you, and my unimportant affection, ever, Henry.

P.S. Soon it will be 1939 and ten years since we talked of Berlin in the bleak Atlantic at our first meeting. I am older and you are wiser and intellectually and spiritually richer.

A letter of December 1937 shows how he could be as enthusiastic about his professional concerns as about his private feelings of friendship, and how he could write about both as it were in the same breath and in one cascade of words:

My dear Charles,

It was inexpressibly satisfactory to get your letter on the eve of Xmas. Letter writing is damnably difficult. I have been working at top speed for two years. Linton and Bottisham Village Colls are completed and working, and Impington, designed by Gropius will start building in a month's time. The latter is a masterpiece.

The Vill. Colls in their various areas are bringing new life into their communities. It is most rewarding to see them at work, especially in the evening, when crowds of young men and women eagerly use all the opportunities for constructive sublimation.[1]

You must read Aldous Huxley's new book 'Ends and Means'. That will reinforce all I hold . . . (and you, I think) . . . as to a rational scientific ordering of the human predicament, divorced from anger and neurosis. No Marxism for me in its undiluted fanatic form. You do not expect too much from any human relationship. Oh, how wise! But woman seems in nearly all cases barred from sharing that wisdom. I think that one of the things that drew me to you more than anything, was the combination of absence of romanticism with real sympathy and humaneness and rationality. I think that even joyous sex gives more with such a background. I go tomorrow to Wiltshire to walk with a group and stay in a modest country house, full of intelligent people with a conscience and humour and a belief in brain and beauty, and devoid of puritanism, but aware of the need for self-organisation.

I wish to God we could meet. I should love it. How can this be? I will send you some articles in the New Year. The year is 1937. How long ago seems the deck of the Aquitania on those cold November evenings in 1929. You have grown inconceivably. Amazing.

Ever yours deeply and unsentimentally,
Henry.

P.S. The Cats? I abominate pets – cats and dogs: they copulate so resignedly.[2]

In May 1938 he is regretting his inability to join Fenn on a trip to the States:

1 Victor Clark, when he was Chief Education Officer of the East Riding, re-members going with Morris one evening to a recently opened community school in the Riding; as they stood outside and watched the people coming in for their various activities, Morris watched in silence, then turned to Clark: 'The word made flesh, Victor,' he said.
2 Fenn has explained that in his previous letter he had referred with delight to two cats he had acquired.

For me it would have been an experience beyond value . . . and in company with you, whom I would choose above everybody, from almost all points of view, to go with . . . when one thinks of the chances of experience and the shortness of life. . . . What frustration! A boon, all the same to be able to write and not to have lost touch (O Aquitania 1929). Swam in the river today at Haslingfield with your spirit still in the offing; beer at seven o'clock at Grantchester. Everything flows – nothing remains except those fragments of true personal relationship. To you I shall always remain bound with ineffaceable precious memories. . . . To you, my closest friend, I send my deepest love – sub specie æternitatis – Henry.

After the war they connected again. Although antipathies came more frequently to the surface, there were still holidays taken together. In a letter in November 1949 he was writing: 'I think we could have one of the most memorable holidays of our lives.' There was a P.S.: 'Twenty years since 1929.' In 1950 they had a holiday in Spain, but Morris was moody, and they clashed. A letter written in December refers to snags encountered: 'Let us not be dragged back into that forgotten Spanish morass! As to my feelings, you are too generous. . . . As ever, all my old affection and admiration, till death do us part! Henry.'

But there were further differences and finally – or penultimately – Fenn wrote from London after Morris had, at the last minute, cancelled an invitation to him to come to Cambridge for a weekend with his girl friend; the letter is undated but it must have been around 1955:

Dear Henry, It seems a pity that our friendship should end in a quarrel; and if I thought it would be of the slightest use I should gladly apologise for contributing to it. But the fact is that I know that we should inevitably quarrel again, and I'm tired of it. . . . So that we shall avoid these upsets, will you agree either not to see me at all, or promise not to suggest weekends. I should be sorry to think that we should not meet at all, but believe me, Henry, I'd prefer that to any more quarrels.

Two years later, when Morris had moved from Cambridge, and things had been put back on a more amicable plane, Fenn, who had developed a serious interest in graphology, sent Morris a reading of his handwriting.

The chief characteristic of this writer is an extraordinary complexity of personality. He is three or four people as the following notes will reveal. Above all he is a person of high aesthetic sense and love of the best in art, music, and literature; love of colour; highly susceptible to visual surroundings. This artistic side of his nature goes along with his impractical side, self consciousness and fussiness about small things. He is imaginative and highly analytical and all this goes with a considerable verbal expressiveness, so he is bound to be a good talker.

He is tremendously energetic, vivacious, enthusiastic; probably irritable and worried (basically, not merely just now). Alert and alive, with a quick active mind: that is always indicated. Then there is a practical man, who can abide by convention, control himself, attend to detail and yearn to be precise and become a perfectionist.

He is honest and sincere, but unreliable because he is erratic. He strives to adapt himself, but often does not (can not?). He is obstinate and may have a temper at times. Impulsive and intuitive. Indications of a passionate nature, offset by determination to be controlled. Humorous (or witty, or both). Independence.

Shortcomings indicated: Selfishness and excessive thrift (which has nothing to do with a generally impulsive tendency to extravagance or are these two sides of the same nature?). Personal secretiveness, the desire to conceal something; this writer can keep a secret well.

Under these typed paragraphs Fenn added, in his own hand:

Dear Henry, Thanks for your letter and invitation which I'm most happy to accept. Please forgive this short answer to your long and so well written letter, but I'm rather preoccupied with work. Regarding the above: I've *tried* to put exactly what seemed to be there – it's not a personal opinion! And I *refuse* to discuss it! Ever, Charles.

Morris never sent the vitriolic reply, which has survived among his papers. It is scribbled, almost illegible, with a quantity of angry crossings out; here it is:

I return your alleged interpretations of my handwriting. I am not in the least concerned to dispute the truth or untruth of them. All I do wish to say is that to put them forward as objective inferences of a 'scientific' character is humbug and a lie. The stench of charlatanism is sickening. You should make a more realistic assessment of the intelligence of your next victim. I forbid you to reply. Any letters of yours will be returned or destroyed unopened. I do not want to be dragged down to your level.

In December 1959 Fenn wrote his last letter to Morris – it is a fitting coda:

I was grieved to hear that you have been so ill. As it happens I wanted to write to you this November a special anniversary letter but had no address, so I wrote to the Pritchards, and asked them to tell you that I should raise a glass to commemorate our 30th year, so to speak.

The letter continued with personal news, but ended:

Henry, I should like to say again that the influence you have had on my life has always been of supreme importance and many of those values I have come to accept as the highest are those to which you first guided me in those days when I seemed to wander around in a partial vacuum. I cannot think of any better way to express my gratitude than to wish you a speedy recovery and a return to the gay electric vitality which you radiated for so many years to so many people.

Such was the muted end of Henry Morris's experience of 'unimportant affection'.

ONE PLUS THREE

Sawston Village College had begun with a flourish in 1928, and had been opened pretentiously in 1930. But things soon began to go wrong. The first warden, A. E. Filsell, left after only two years, possibly because he objected to Morris hovering over him and over the college. His successor, J. G. Milner, disliked Morris, quarrelled with him, and on retiring from the wardenship in 1945 became a county councillor and governor of the college. From this vantage point, not lacking allies, he continued to attack Morris until the latter retired from the service of the county council. Other local troubles have already been described in Chapter 4.

But troubles at Sawston did not deter Morris from going ahead with his plans for three more colleges. In letters to Fenn we can follow the process from its initial stages, through to the three completed buildings.

May 1934. I've just got off an appeal to the Carnegie Trustees for £10,000 towards the cost of three more village colleges.

November 1934. Fortunately, we have decided to put up three more village colleges and I'm engaged all my working hours thinking out the architecture and equipment. I had Gropius, the German architect, staying with me a few weeks ago (with a wife, exceptionally beautiful and equally intelligent – marvellous combination), and his conversation and many months of study of modern architectural techniques, confirm me in the necessity of doing all contemporary buildings without regard to traditional style.

December 1934. I have just secured £3000 from the Carnegie Trustees for parts of our three new village colleges, which are to cost £50,000.

October 1936. I had to cut my holiday short in view of the need for securing the Histon V.C. Scheme.[1] A site of twelve acres has been given by Chivers, and they have given £6000 in cash. The building is to cost £30,000 and Gropius has produced a wonderful plan which will be the most advanced rural community centre in this country. Meantime Bottisham Village College will be finished in January when it will be opened by the Education Minister, and Linton Village College will be finished in March. I shall feel

1 The original name for Impington Village College.

then that with four V.C.'s the idea is permanently safe. I read a paper on the subject at the September meeting of the British Association at Blackpool [5] and went off the deepend.

22nd January 1937. I am in a sea of troubles with the Gropius scheme. He is shortly to go (this is very confidential) as Professor of Architecture to Harvard. So U.S.A. gets him. I think I shall finally pull off G's scheme, but it will be difficult.

22nd December 1937. Linton and Bottisham Vill. Colls. are completed and working; and Impington will start building in a month's time. The latter is a masterpeice.

6th February 1939. Gropius' building is almost finished and will be opened by Lord Baldwin (!) Chancellor to the University, in September next. . . . It will I believe be the most distinguished modern building in Britain.

So much for the skeleton history of the next three village colleges. He was determined that after Sawston the next three colleges should reflect his new found interest in the productions of living artists and contemporary architects and designers. So the conventional Georgian symmetry of Sawston was rejected and new men were encouraged to become involved in his plans, not only for the village colleges, and other new schools, but also for the renovation of old ones, in which he took a great pride. H. L. Fenn (not related to Charles) who taught at Linton Village College and later became an HMI has pointed out: 'Contrary to general belief he did not forget the village primary schools, many of which he changed from County Council green or municipal brown to gay and exhilarating colours. Furniture was designed for particular use in class-rooms and practical rooms and he encouraged teachers to come forward with new ideas.' He was always keen that visitors to Bottisham should see not only the college, but that they should also inspect the new and sparkling village primary school there. In a junior school at Swavesey he was enthusiastic about the blue tiling, selected by himself, and was particularly proud of what had once been a drab Church of England school at Great Wilbraham, which was transformed into a gay and delightful place and which became a show piece, with its enlarged windows, white dining room and blue doors.

SHIFT OF TASTE

The transformation of his taste – perhaps conversion is a more appropriate word – came about slowly. In his early days in Trinity Street his furniture (which included some eighteenth-century reproduction pieces) and the decoration of his flat were later echoed in the neo-Georgian designs for Sawston; originally both Sawston and his flat had coloured reproductions of French Impressionists on the walls. But gradually changes occurred, and almost always as a direct result of some personal contact; perhaps a meeting with an influential artist or because a friend had introduced him to some new work. Often he followed up the experience by persuading such contacts, or other experts or artists, actually to execute something for him or for one of his schools: to paint a picture, carve a figure, advise on colours, design some furniture, or (as in the case of Gropius), a village college.

Probably his first contact with someone who knew about and enthusiastically enjoyed the contemporary visual arts was with Mansfield Forbes, an eccentric and lively English don from Clare. He was fascinated by Celtic art and culture and knew a great deal about medieval Scottish architecture; he had friends who were rising young architects; he was a brilliant lecturer and a great talker and walker. He and Morris would walk out to Grantchester on Sundays. They became good friends. Forbes redesigned the interior of his own Victorian house on the Backs, 'Finella'; here he experimented with new materials, and introduced conscious oddities – the lavatory lined with black glass, a tiled wall in the hall, a statue enclosed in glass and washed by a perpetual fountain. But in spite of the new materials, the whole thing had something of a *fin de siècle* air. Morris was clearly not ready to be influenced by Forbes's visual ideas. In 1928 their friendship ended childishly and dramatically; Forbes called on Morris late one night, failed to rouse him with shouts and threw a dustbin lid through his window. Morris did not think this funny, wrote him a note saying that his eccentricity was too much, and that all was over between them. They never came together again. Forbes died in 1934.

At the time of the opening of Sawston in 1930, Robert Wellington, who had been introduced to him in Cambridge and was working in the Zwemmer Gallery in London, remembers him rushing up from Cambridge to return laden with dozens of coloured reproductions of Impressionists to cover the walls of the public rooms for the Prince of Wales's official visit to Sawston. Morris returned often to Zwemmer's, and became interested in original paintings and, through Wellington, got to know a number of young painters and their work. Discussions with them and with dealers gradually brought home to him the importance of originals and weaned him away from colour reproductions. Typically his newfound enthusiasm resulted in action, for he was instrumental, through encouragement and financial backing, in getting Robert Wellington with John Piper to found 'Contemporary Lithographs Ltd' in 1935 – one of the first enterprises which set out to make original works of living artists available cheaply to schools. The first set of lithographs included pictures by John Piper, Barnett Freedman, Paul and John Nash, Robert Medley and Eric Ravilious. They were sold to local education authorities and schools at a special discount.

In the end he became obsessed with the importance of keeping colour reproductions shut up in portfolios, from where they might occasionally be taken out and looked at, but never hung. He was once asked by members of the education committee of another authority if he would come and advise them on schemes for rural reconstruction. The meeting was to take place in one of their new schools. Seeing some reproductions on the wall of the entrance hall, he commented: 'You know, I'd rather see a dead cat on the wall than a reproduction.' His hosts, from that moment, were not impressed by his advice.

Friends helped to select the colour schemes for new schools. Lord Fairhaven, the first Chairman of the Governors of Bottisham and a member of the Education Committee, was something of a connoisseur and a collector. Morris asked him to choose the colours for the classrooms of the new college. Morris's comment on the proposed art room, painted a pale mauve, was not polite: 'Looks like a tart's bedroom,' he said. But he was never a respecter of mere rank. He was more respectful of the choices of colours for Linton Village College made by Møholy Nagy on his way to America from the wreck of the Bauhaus. And Morris himself could be seen – as I once saw him in the new but unfinished Girls' High School in Cambridge – mixing paints in a bucket in a bare classroom, trying them out on the walls, and then instructing the foreman to make up a particular colour that appealed to him. He also used local talent. Loughnan Pendred, a woodcarver who taught at Bottisham as the master in charge of Design and Crafts ('that was the name for the woodwork master', he explains) was commissioned by Morris to do a long carved panel for what was, and still is, called 'the Blue Room'. He writes:

This work took me over a year to finish, and Morris used often to visit us to see how it was getting on. At first he was disappointed because it was not like a Henry Moore, then the up and coming sculptor. I had to point out tactfully that not being Henry Moore I could only produce a Pendred. However when the Bauhaus was closed and some of its members came to England, he brought Møholy Nagy to see us. Møholy Nagy seemed pleased with the panel and said it reminded him of Ernst Barlach's work; Morris immediately came round and accepted it as a work of art – probably much more than this early work of mine deserved. I think, in the matter of art, he was apt to be swayed by what he thought he ought to like. I hope I don't malign him there.

JACK PRITCHARD, CATALYST

Probably the most powerful direct influence on his 'conversion', and indirectly on the development of British architecture was Jack Pritchard, who got to know Morris well in Cambridge in the early twenties. Morris was the newly appointed Assistant Education Secretary, and Pritchard an ex-navy undergraduate reading engineering and economics. They remained close friends until Morris's death. When he left Cambridge, Pritchard went into a variety of jobs, ending up in furniture manufacture. This involved him in the use of new materials, such as plywood, which new industrial and scientific techniques were increasingly making available. Thus he came into contact with the experimental ideas of designers, craftsmen and architects in Scandinavia and Germany, and in particular with those of the Bauhaus School of Architecture at Weimar. The director of the Bauhaus,

1 Student, 1911   2 Soldier, 1915

3 "You should have seen him at the opening of Sawston." (p. 43)

4 Sitting room at the Old Granary.

5 Sawston Village College.

6 The entrance to Impington Village College.

7 Henry Morris in 1958.

Walter Gropius, had introduced a new and expanded concept of architectural design and training by bringing together artists, craftsmen, engineers and planners to work in a team with the architect, all concerned with the total impact their work would make on the whole environment as it would be felt by those who were to live and move within it. In the 1920s and early '30s the Bauhaus was the fountain head of the modern movement in architecture and the related arts, starting where William Morris had left off. Bauhaus students therefore looked on science, engineering and industry as godsends, not enemies, as means to be used and welcomed by the artist and designer. This led to constant experiment with the multitude of new materials which the scientific revolution was making available.

Pritchard's outlook and taste were deeply influenced by such ideas and experiments, and he had been disappointed by the conventional design and appearance of Sawston, while being enthusiastic about Morris's idea of the village college. He remembers however that already while Sawston was being built that Morris began to modify his outlook, and to use a new phrase: 'There must be no regrets for the past'. By this he wanted to stress the importance of looking forward, not only in planning, but in the visual and architectural expression of his plans. This pointed to the employment of contemporary models and if possible contemporary architects for the building of schools.

Therefore Pritchard's contact with the few British architects of the time who could be called 'contemporary', and who were familiar with Bauhaus ideas and practice, was of immediate relevance for Morris. Pritchard knew Maxwell Fry well and had commissioned Wells Coates to design for him the Lawn Road Flats in Belsize Park in 1933. Here in his own rooftop flat, he introduced Walter Gropius to Henry Morris in 1934.

Pritchard had been directly instrumental in bringing Gropius out of Hitler's Germany where, because of his liberal ideas which he insisted on expressing, he risked not only official displeasure but arrest. He arranged for Gropius to meet a number of British architects, but it was the introduction to Morris which was historic. Pritchard was a catalyst promoting an explosive but benign reaction, which he described vividly: 'Enlightened architect met enlightened educationist; result: orgasm.' For Morris and Gropius got on well, and admiration was mutual. 'I remember he succeeded in loosing my tongue in our architectural discussions in spite of my poor stuttering English' Gropius wrote to Pritchard after Morris's death, and went on: 'His Village College was a true creative idea, still full of potentialities. I have never quite understood why the British authorities did not give him the green light. . . . An inspiring friend has left us.'

Following this first meeting Morris became seized with the desire to get Gropius to design Impington. When Gropius, cooperating with Maxwell Fry, agreed to do this at a knock down fee one step only had been taken towards its fulfilment. The next move was blocked. The Education Committee objected to the architects' fee of

£1200, when they could have used their own architect for nothing. Pritchard and Morris felt that too much was at stake to allow this objection to stand. They decided to raise the money somehow; they had exactly three weeks to do it in; letters appeared in the Press,[1] they approached friends and Trusts; within a fortnight contributions amounted to nearly £600. Together they decided themselves to guarantee the remainder. The County Council accepted the designs of Gropius and Fry, and the money. The first hurdle was passed: there were others ahead.

One great regret for Morris was his failure to acquire a sculpture by Henry Moore for Impington. Moore at that time was not a fashionable artist; the general public found his work shocking. Morris went to see him; they discussed the idea of the village college and Moore agreed to attempt a major sculpture which would stand in front of Gropius's Impington. In a foreword to *The Story of Digswell* [26] Moore generously acknowledged Morris's influence on him and on other artists who were involved in work for the village colleges. 'In my own case, the Family Group in its differing forms sprang from my absorbing his idea of the village college – that it should be an institution which could provide for the family at all its stages.'

The first maquette of the Family Group was sent to Morris, who was eager to have it executed. But for the Cambridgeshire county councillors of the time, Moore, and the price asked, were too much. They refused to order it. After the war, much to Morris's annoyance, the Hertfordshire County Council bought The Family Group for one of their new schools in Stevenage.

1 *New Statesman*, 25 April 1936.

The trouble over the architects' fee, and the disappointment over the Henry Moore were all in keeping with the stormy gestation period and ominous birth of Impington Village College. In 1930 W. B. Chivers, of Histon, offered the first gift of twelve acres of parkland at Impington, for the building of a village college. The Cottenham Parish Council immediately protested that the next college should be at Cottenham, a village a few miles away from Impington. The embryonic dispute was dropped in 1931 because of the economic crisis; a ban was placed on all school building. In 1934 when school building began again Chivers offered a further 13 acres of land. Cottenham and other villages again protested. In 1935, in an attempt to pacify all parties, the Education Committee asked Morris to prepare an alternative scheme involving two smaller colleges, one at Impington, one at Cottenham. This was turned down by the Board of Education which favoured Impington. Immediately Chivers offered a gift of £6000 for an adult wing.

By 1937 the situation had become serious. In a letter to Leonard Elmhirst, dated 18 January, Morris described it as desperate. In this letter it is interesting and surprising, to hear the note of sympathy and understanding he felt for his chairman, and for the 'farmers and conservative squires' who were his masters.

May I send you a note about Gropius' scheme for the Village College at Impington, which we are planning for a model of what a rural community centre might be. In his attempt to meet the requirements of finance, Gropius has drawn up no less than six schemes, most of which involved shedding various features which we hoped to include. The sixth and I hope the last scheme is now before us, and any further reduction in the accommodation would destroy its role as a model for the rest of the country.

The situation is a desperate one. The Education Committee are only prepared to go on with the scheme if their liability is limited to approximately £20,000. My chairman is not prepared to go to the Council except on this basis. He is in a difficult position. If the Council provided a building for Senior School purposes only (which is all they are required to do by statute), they need not spend more than £13,000. They have been willing to go beyond their statutory obligations, and provide approximately 50 per cent more funds out of their resources. I think it is remarkable that a small and poor county should do this.

This week the County Finance Committee met and they have advised the council to refer back all capital expenditure, including the Impington scheme, and there is a suggestion to shelve it. This has given our reactionaries an opportunity and they are in full pursuit. But I am anxious to save the scheme for many reasons. I want to see Gropius' scheme carried out, partly as an expression on English soil, of his genius, partly as an example of educational building, and a stimulus to the rest of the Local Education Authorities of England; partly to show what a rural community centre might do, in providing education and recreation for the whole community of all ages, partly to show what we can get if, in State Education, we use outside architects instead of official architects.

I write to you with deep reluctance, but I compel myself to do so because of the importance of Gropius' scheme for the State system of Education. If it can be carried out, it will be one of the most significant advances in State education in the post war period – all the more so as it will be under the aegis of a rural County Council of farmers and conservative country squires.

Elmhirst was unable to help this time, but in his reply referred to the contribution he had already made, anonymously it seems, to the appeal for help with the architects' fee, which had been an essential first step towards the building of Impington.

In that same spring of 1937 the parish pump squabbles of earlier days were being renewed. In February the Parish Council of Cottenham, joining with the school managers and others wrote to the Education Committee, once again pointing out that Impington was not suitable for a village college because it is so near Cambridge; that 'certain gifts in money and kind have been offered towards the erection of a proposed Village College at Impington'. And protesting that 'private patronage should not be allowed to dictate public policy'. There was a further objection that Impington was mainly an urban community, while Cottenham was truly rural. Cottenham was supported by other Parish Councils, including Milton, where in March 1937 the Chairman, Councillor R. M. Woodman, also signed the supporting letter; this recommended that 'a halt should be called to the building of Village Colleges to see if those already built justify the expenditure'. In April the same councillor, in committee, moved that 'the erection of further Village Colleges be postponed for the lifetime of the present council'. The motion was defeated by fifteen votes to three.

Three months later approval was given by the Board of Education and in the December meeting of the Education Committee it was reported that gifts of £11,000 had been received towards the cost of Impington Village College, leaving the County Council £10,000 to find, this being matched by the grant from the government. A tender was accepted, and work authorised to start.

Unlike Sawston, Impington Village College opened without pomp at the end of 1939. But also unlike Sawston, the early years were auspicious; partly no doubt because of the war, there was a marked lack of local feuds and jealousies. And in spite of there being no trumpeted opening ceremony, no cutting of tapes and unveiling of plaques, the new building could not avoid, over the following months and years, commanding the attention of architects, educationists, artists and critics. Linton and Bottisham had contained many new features. They had been designed by the county architect, S. E. Urwin, working, not always happily, under the constant eye of Henry Morris. But the building of Impington was conceived by an architect of international fame, who took delight in translating what he recognised as a great idea into a building suitably sited, designed and furnished.

The college is set among trees, and a great chestnut tree in the front is framed by the curved upper windows at the end of the fan-shaped hall. The adult wing containing club rooms and seminar rooms, curves gently to the left; stretching away at the back, overlooking fields, are the classrooms of the senior school. The outstanding feature is the great corridor, the concourse 140 feet long and 20 feet wide, which is more than just a place to move through, or across, from school to hall, from hall to adult wing; it is a rendezvous point, an exhibition hall, a bar or a dining hall; whether being used as a centre or a passage it is a place where young and old, teachers and taught, athletes, actors and students can meet and talk and pass on their way.

Nicholas Pevsner's notes on Impington in the Cambridgeshire volume of his *Buildings of England* series [36] bring out its qualities, its influence, and the probable source of its inspiration:

Impington Village College 1938, by Walter Gropius and Maxwell Fry. One of the best buildings of its date in England, if not the best. Equally successful in its grouping and setting among the trees of Impington Hall Estate. The pattern for much to come (including most of the progressive schools built after the Second World War), insofar as at Impington the practical and visual advantages of modern forms in a loose yet coherent, completely free-looking arrangement had first been demonstrated. Can it have been the effect of English picturesque notions on the more rigid intellect of Gropius? As for this loose grouping as such, it must however be said that the village colleges preceding Impington had already used this device, though without the full realisation of its aesthetic possibilities. . . . Perhaps it originated in the mind of Henry Morris, whose idea the Village Colleges had been.

Herbert Read was another critic and artist who was entranced and impressed by Impington, and recognised, in his reference to it in his *Education Through Art* [40A] that Gropius and Morris together had created something which justified the title of his book:

Is it possible not merely to conceive, but to build and introduce into the existing educational system, schools which provide the essentials of an educative environment? The answer is yes; it has been done at least in one instance, and a model . . . does exist on English soil. This is the Village College at Impington, in Cambridgeshire.

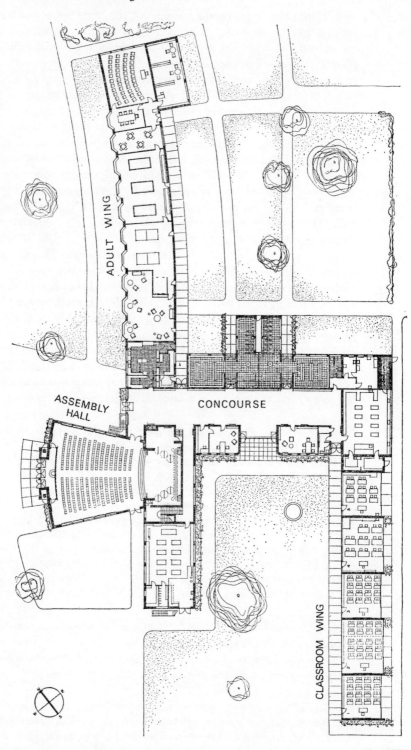

Ground floor plan of Impington Village College

Finally, Paul Reilly, architectural critic, writing in the *Manchester Guardian* of 18 July 1942, noted among other things:

THE LESSON OF IMPINGTON
In the last few years the Cambridge university buildings have doubled or trebled in extent . . . yet sadder and sadder are the results. Heavy pretentiousness is the general note. Streets of laboratories would do discredit to the warehouse districts of Manchester or Liverpool. Impington College therefore, clean and elegant, a mile or two out of town, yet hardly known to the average don or undergraduate, is not only a social phenomenon of immense importance, but an aesthetic one too.

Slowly the lesson of Impington was learnt, even by Cambridge dons, for, as Pevsner says: 'Impington was the pattern of much to come.' This opinion was echoed by Bryan Robertson in 1967 in his introduction to a catalogue of original paintings for schools being shown in the Whitechapel Art Gallery of which he was at the time director. He wrote: 'By commissioning Gropius to build a village college at Impington in the 1930's, when no modern architect of this calibre had been used to build a school in England before, Morris made history in English education.'

THE POTENTIAL OF LOCAL GOVERNMENT

As soon as the waves of London evacuees had been settled by teachers and welfare workers in the villages and schools of Cambridgeshire, Morris faced a long period when his skill as a pragmatic administrator, as a brilliant beggar and as a visionary planner would no longer be immediately usable. But he was still a constructive idealist, and the fountain of his creative thinking could not suddenly be turned off. So he took up an interest which he had harboured for many years but which, until the wartime interlude gave him some leisure, he had not allowed to expand: an interest in the whole political and social structure of English education, and more particularly, in the actual curriculum imposed by the school on the child.

The opportunity to expand this interest was offered by his own professional colleagues in local government, the Association of Directors and Secretaries for Education. They, like most people not immediately concerned with fighting the war, turned their attention seriously, and early, to the problems of 'postwar reconstruction'. They decided to come together and to make their views known in a report to the Board of Education, which was to be called 'The Orange Book' [25]. As soon as he heard of the idea, he urged his colleagues in a memorandum, 'Postwar Policy in Education', dated July 1941,[1] [7] to make their voices heard, not only in the corridors of Whitehall but among the wider public also. In making this plea he was eager to bring to their attention the fact that constitutionally, as a professional body, they were in a much stronger position than any group of civil servants, to formulate policies and pursue them. Typically he began the paper he wrote for the Association with a quotation from Keats: 'We are standing on the forehead of the years to come' and went on:

The Officers of Local Education Authorities should make a major and independent contribution to the elaboration of the educational system that will serve England for the second half of the twentieth century. We ought

---

1 The quotations in this chapter all come from this memorandum unless otherwise noted.

not, I submit, to be content to be dragged at the heels of the Board of Education as mere accessories, and for very good solid reasons. The Board is a Government body which cannot go beyond the limits laid down by a Minister responsible to the Cabinet, itself responsible to a many-minded Parliament. The Education Officers, as a body are not constitutionally conditioned in this way. Speaking as a body they can express views of policy such as could not be expected of an individual officer, and they have more freedom than the Board. In this circumstance alone, the Association is in a powerful position both strategically and tactically.

The Association, reflecting the experience and thought of local government in education, can take the decisive and original lead in educational policy. If it does so, nothing will more effectively justify local government in education. . . . We should produce, not a memorandum, but a comprehensive report on post-war policy which . . . could be circulated throughout the country far and wide, with the intention of informing and indeed creating public opinion – in the House of Commons, amongst teachers, in all the professions, amongst leaders of commerce, skilled workers etc., etc. Such a document would have to be written, not in the administrative English of memoranda, but in literary idiomatic English . . . it could be well printed with the format of a Penguin Special – and indeed must be printed at the price of sixpence and circulated by the ten thousand. . . . We ought not, I suggest, to hesitate about going to the public. We have been able, in the past at least, to get an educational policy; we have failed in not getting the backing of public opinion.

In addressing his colleagues in this way, Morris was voicing a new idea: that administrators, and local government administrators at that, were justified in 'creating' public opinion to support their policies. He was also emphasising his faith in the concept of state education as found in Britain, where the schools are locally administered and only in part financed – and therefore only in part controlled – by central government. But although he liked the concept of state education he did not like the name.

It is more accurate to refer to Community Education, for we want a phrase that does justice to the fact that public education is provided by elected local authorities and that the Board of Education is a partner in the matter. . . . We tend to forget that local government is a cornerstone of freedom, as every dictator realises when, on getting into power he abolishes it. (Napoleon in France, Mussolini in Italy, Hitler in Germany.)

BASIS FOR CURRICULUM REFORM

Far-reaching and far-sighted suggestions for curriculum reform in the post primary schools formed the weightiest section of his contribution. Already he saw the problem comprehensively, that is to say he took into consideration the whole intelligence range of the age group from eleven to sixteen. He was therefore facing the major problem of what to offer the average child long before John Newsom put his name to *Half Our Future*.[1] Morris's proposals are striking because of the realism he injected into them. This may well have surprised some of his colleagues, for probably none of them was aware that this realism was rooted in his own childhood experience. As a chief officer he was surely exceptional in that he had himself attended an elementary school until the age of fourteen, which he then left in order to go to work. He knew what it was like to be branded an 'early leaver', to be an educational reject of the system. As a little boy in Southport he had no doubt sat in large classes, been forced to listen for hours on end to unsuitable and unpalatable lessons mechanically taught by uninspired teachers. Once again therefore, just as the experience of his childhood and youth contributed to his ideas for the village college, so this experience contributed strongly to his dissatisfaction with the traditional school curriculum.

The intellectual sources of his ideas about curriculum reform are harder to trace. The influence of Hastings Rashdall is discernible in his insistence that the school experience of the adolescent should seek to feed the emotions as generously as it strove to feed the mind. Of the Middle Ages, Rashdall had written:

The academic discipline trained pure intellect, encouraged habits of laborious subtlety, heroic industry, and intense application, while it left uncultivated the imagination, the taste and a sense of beauty – all the amenities of a civilised intellect. It taught men to think and to work rather than to enjoy. Most of what we understand by culture, much of what Aristotle understood as the noble use of leisure was unappreciated by the medieval intellect [39].

At the same time a number of new theories associated with the name of John Dewey were being tried out in the United States. Morris must have been aware of them. John Dewey's doctrine, and its application to the school, which would form an integrated element of the local community would surely have appealed to him; but there is no reference to Dewey in his writings nor in his extant speeches. He did, however, at an early date, acknowledge the importance of Sanderson of Oundle. He approved of the system by which pupils at Oundle were introduced to theory through practice, and by which engineering, the crafts and other practical subjects were given the same status as academic subjects. In an article in the *Education Handbook* [10], he noted that Sanderson was 'always stretching forward to the realisation of the school as a microcosm of actual life, for schools according to Sanderson, should be miniature copies of the world'.

As early as 1923, in the opening paragraph of the Cambridgeshire Report on the teaching of Religion in Schools, he had commended Sanderson:

The ambition of teachers is enlarged of late. No longer are they content to

1 Report of the Central Advisory Council for Education, HMSO 1963.

impart information. . . . Some, like Sanderson of Oundle . . . see no time to spare on exercises of mere preparation. . . . The pupil must learn his proper craft by working at it, as in the old days of apprenticeship. Indeed the school is the ideal workshop.

THE PEDAGOGIC FALLACY

Morris had a habit of lifting phrases and whole paragraphs from articles and papers he had written years before. At this time however, a new phrase emerged: the pedagogic fallacy. This he defined as the tendency teachers have of trying to educate adolescents with exercises, texts, and materials suitable only for people who have reached a sophisticated degree of maturity, or only for very exceptional and gifted younger pupils. He made the point most clearly in a broadcast he gave on the North American Service of the BBC in September 1942 [9]:

For twenty years I have been fired by the belief that the school in England, and indeed in every country in the world, has to be re-made. The school has been dominated by the needs of the 'brainy' boy or girl, who is good at books and comes out well in examinations, and who wins prizes at the university. For millions of boys and girls who learn by practice and action this is a gigantic error.

The 'remaking' or 'reorganising' of our schools has gathered momentum in the second half of this century. These organisational moves have been accompanied by new thoughts about the curriculum, and here one principle has been gaining ground, the idea that the education of the child cannot be thought of in isolation from the education of the adult. This was clearly seen by Morris, who explained that the pedagogic fallacy could be overcome only through extending the provision of education from childhood to youth and maturity.

Only after a ubiquitous and fully articulated system of adult education has been established can we afford to reform the curriculum followed by children, for only then would we be justified in persuading teachers to abandon their fallacy, having the assurance that time and opportunity was available at a more appropriate moment in their lives, for those things which are desirable, but for which few children are ready.

Primary school teachers had already made important reforms in the curriculum for infants and juniors and, he contended, the resulting decrease in child misery and increase in child happiness had been enormous. But those concerned with post-primary education had so far failed to learn from this revolution, and he called for an effort to

discover by research those art forms, whether of novel or story, of music or picture, which are appropriate to this age group, and contemporary artists must be asked to create new forms for them. . . . For the education of the adolescent ought to be given in terms of the experience and instincts of the adolescent.

THE ADOLESCENTS' CURRICULUM

Morris reminded his colleagues of the 'process of unimaginative cruelty' by which children between the ages of fourteen and sixteen were introduced to *King Lear* and *Macbeth*, and made to 'study' *Paradise Lost* and the poems of Wordsworth, Keats and Shelley. He pointed out that 'consciousness of the art of poetry is not shared by a large number of people . . . and only occurs after the age of about sixteen, even among the most sensitive; and even then it is of the less subtle forms of poetry. The period of the deepening and development of poetic taste is between eighteen and thirty'. He quoted Herbert Read's autobiography, to bear him out:

It was not until my seventeenth year that I became conscious of the art of poetry. At school we read and even acted Shakespeare and there were 'recitations' which must have included some verse, but I never read a volume of poems by choice. . . . The very abstractness of Shelley's poetry kept me at a distance. Shelley I would now say demands a degree of intellectual development which I did not reach by the age of seventeen or eighteen. Tennyson was more open to my simple sensibility [40].

For further support he enlisted Havelock Ellis – describing him as 'one of the greatest humanists of our time, who was also one of the gentlest and most deeply religious of men'. Ellis had written:

There are many infuriating aspects of modern education. One such specially arouses my own fury. That is the widespread custom of introducing into the school-room, to be thumbed by innocent children, the sublimest works of human imagination. Little is thought of reducing to the level of mere school-books Shakespeare and Marlowe and Milton to sicken children who as yet can know nothing of the naked ecstacies and anguish which are here expressed and transformed into redeeming shapes of immortal beauty.

The Bible, for those who truly know it, is among such works of divine art, and it is the Bible, above all, which is thrust on to children who would find far more spiritual nourishment, if not in Hans Andersen's Fairy Tales, at all events in books of natural history such as K. De Schweintz's *How a Baby is Born*.

Where the superior officials are found who, against the judgement of many of the best teachers, ordain that children should acquire a life-long disgust for great literature . . . I do not know . . . But until they are mercifully confined to homes for Mental Defectives, the world is not likely to 'rediscover the Bible' [30].

Morris insisted of course that it was not only in the teaching of literature that the pedagogic fallacy was rife; he spent several paragraphs attacking the Board of Education's *Handbook of Suggestions for Teachers* (1937) for spreading the assumption that 'boys and girls under the age of fourteen in our elementary schools, can be taught in the terms of the culture and concepts of adult maturity'. He took as an example the section on History (33 pages long) and by extensive quotation showed how ludicrous and unrealistic were the expectations of the HMI's or the teachers responsible for it.

The authors expected the child, on leaving school at fourteen, to have 'some idea of the stage in world history when British history begins . . . of the main social and economic changes through which the country has passed in the last thousand years . . . of the development of the national system of government, of the growth of the Empire, and of the present position of the British Commonwealth' [5]. Morris then broadened his attack: 'The assumption that a child of between eleven and fourteen or indeed fifteen is intellectually aesthetically and morally a grown-up person appears in many other sections of this book, and the same assumption pervades the whole series of other Reports – Hadow, Spens and the various specialist reports in the secondary school curriculum.'

He draws attention to the important and unavoidable connection between inappropriate school curricula and the inappropriate examination syllabuses. Here 'the Pedagogic Fallacy of projecting the intellectual and aesthetic understanding of maturity into the minds and personalities of young people . . . is found complete. A critical treatise on the (public) examination syllabuses would clear away vast oppressive masses of human folly in English secondary education.'

Having exposed the pedagogic fallacy, he urged the reform of the traditional way in which lessons were presented by teachers, calling for a lifting of the oppressive mechanical atmosphere to be felt, seen and heard in the classrooms of England. He sympathised with the naturally active children as they sat still and largely silent, at their iron-legged desks, listening, or pretending to listen, to a teacher. For the adolescent, opportunities should be provided for new kinds of action and pursuits which often are better carried on outside the classroom. At a time when the Boy Scouts were becoming a matter for derision among intellectuals, he was not afraid to praise the genius of Baden Powell for seeing the need for and establishing the Movement, which, as he said in a speech to the Conference of the Town and Country Planning Association in April 1946 [15] 'did nothing more and nothing less than recognise the physical and instinctive stage which the boy had reached, and then set out to meet his physical and instinctive needs'. He would recall, without sentimentality, the meaningful boyhood experienced in the past by the sons of fishermen or farmers, educated largely out of school and out of the reach of pedagogues, and learning about life in the world of action. In looking back like this he was at the same time looking forward, and using the example of the unschooled but educated apprentice of the past to point the way to an extension of education in the future, beyond and outside the school:

When I speak of the extension of education, I do not mean merely the extension of formal education by instruction and discourse. We are so ridden by departmental views of education, so prone to look upon education as a parenthesis in the human adventure, that in thinking about education we think solely of the school.

In another paper 'The Post Primary Curriculum' [8] he gave a prophetic warning that even intellectuals might eventually lose faith in universal schooling:

A disabling weakness of the post-primary school is its isolation and its divorce from the real world of action with which children in late adolescence are striving to make acquaintance. Unless this divorce can be got over, the desirability of full time schooling for all adolescents everywhere will be questioned, or denied, even in liberal and enlightened quarters. We have to discover the contemporary equivalent to that element of reality which was provided by the apprenticeship system.

He wrote with passion about the inappropriateness of the school experience offered to the majority of children:

Our State educational institutions and particularly our schools are class-room ridden, lesson ridden, textbook ridden, information ridden and given over to incessant didactic discourse and discursiveness. Even in the best schools . . . the element of discourse is overwhelming [24].
  Thus, in Education, of all places, the miracle is reversed, and the wine of Art is turned into the Water of discourse [7].

And he uttered a realistic threat to his colleagues that the post-war raising of the school leaving age (which he insisted should be sixteen) would prove 'a gigantic disappointment and failure', unless it was accompanied by a radical re-orientation of the content and method of post primary education. And he underlined his point by a quotation from T. S. Eliot's 'The Rock':

> All our knowledge brings us nearer to our ignorance
> All our ignorance brings us nearer to death . . .
> Where is the life we have lost in living?
> Where is the wisdom we have lost in knowledge?
> Where is the knowledge we have lost in information?

There were some hopeful signs. There had been a time when Art in grammar schools had been called 'a relief subject', and in some schools, for instance at Impington Village College, things were changing already. The following is from his broadcast to North America in 1942.

The secret of the Senior School is Activity – the major road to knowledge both for children and grown ups. Here (at Impington Village College) the dismal reign of chalk and talk, of the mechanical use of textbooks and the piling up of parrot facts unrelated to the child's experience is finished.

The school has become a society with a way of life, a hive of constructiveness. One group is in the 6 acre garden, with its adjacent laboratory and greenhouse. Here all kinds of fruit and vegetables are grown for experiment and demonstration. Seeds and manures are tested, accounts and records carefully kept . . .

I always feel that the midday meal can be one of the most significant incidents in the life of the Senior School. The common meal has been one of the main instruments of education in civilisation east and west. It is not an extra at Impington. It has a place of honour in the curriculum. The tables are charmingly set out; there is a fine sung grace, the children sit together with their teachers, there is an interval between the courses ('Slowness is beauty' said Rodin). . . . Here is a scene of happiness, gaiety and health [9].

He summed up his ideas for presenting the arts to adolescents by saying that the arts should, like games, be free from discourse and from examination pressure and be so organised that the practice or experience of music or dancing, drama or painting or poetry should be enjoyed by the young and looked forward to like games periods after Latin or Maths. Like the skills, like religion or food or bodily exercise, he contended that the arts are a necessary nourishment for human beings, hence a necessity for a full life. Schools therefore should set out to initiate children into enjoying the arts, not passively but through active and creative work.

Such suggestions and others for the reform of the curriculum and of teaching style take up the bulk of the paper he presented to his colleagues, but at the end he moved on to wider fields. All his suggestions about the curriculum assumed not only that the school leaving age would be raised to sixteen, but also (foreseeing the county colleges of the Butler Act) that Day Continuation Schools or Further Education Colleges would be set up to provide part-time education for those between sixteen and eighteen years old.

In the paper which he wrote on the post primary curriculum he was at pains to draw a distinction between the needs of adolescents under sixteen, and the needs of young men and women in their later teens. Another distinction which was to become a major issue in the 1950s and '60s, the division between the experience of young people selected for grammar schools and those going to non-selective schools worried him much less. For he saw this distinction being overcome, not so much through the institution of comprehensive schools (this alone, as we now know, is not enough) but through the reorganisation of teaching strategies, such as have been realised in the more successful comprehensive schools of the 1970s: that is through the introduction of individual learning, and through a great extension of library resources in schools.

He insisted that the child who was not suited to a grammar school experience should not be fed on the scraps and leavings of his grammar school contemporaries, but he was realistic about the intelligent few, the 'able minority who should be trained to take the intellectual lead in the universities, the professions, in administration etc.' He recognised that among the able minority there would be some who would want to start earlier than sixteen on their special courses. They should have every opportunity to develop their interests, both through contact with suitable teachers and through greatly increased provision of libraries:

All schools, through their libraries, must increasingly provide for the service of access. In the library, double or treble its conventional size, all children should be able to approach the written word and the illustrated world at their own particular level. For the abler children this is doubly important since they will be enabled to do what is done by the child in the lucky home, take down the *Republic*, or Dante, or Eddington, or *Tom Jones* or Hogarth or Botticelli etc . . . the point is that they will do this spontaneously, of their own free will.

A COMMON NATIONAL SYSTEM

Given the raising of the school leaving age to sixteen, given the reformed curriculum for secondary schools, and given the provision of separate education for all over the age of sixteen, either full-time in sixth form colleges or part-time in county colleges, the selection procedure at eleven-plus would become unnecessary, and a common system of education could result. From this system he specifically excluded the public schools. He disapproved of them partly because, being isolated from the local community and confined to one sex and one social class, they blinkered their pupils, but above all because they were socially divisive. He therefore stipulated their exclusion from the state system, not because he was happy to accept their continuing existence, nor because he was unaware of their power and importance – on the contrary. He wanted the Association to take a firm, anti-public-school stand and he made no attempt to disguise his disapproval of the privileged baronial position which the public schools had won in the nineteenth century and which they still clung to:

Part of the case, and the most profoundly important part of the case against the public schools is moral. The English nation . . . has been riven into two nations not on any principle . . . based on, say, virtue and intelligence, but on a material principle based on money. . . . It should be stated without qualification and equivocation that, (a) the basis of the public school system is financial, (b) that it is in demand, not primarily because it cultivates intelligence and inculcates virtue, but primarily because it significates the individual on the basis of a principle of exclusion. Thousands of guileless boys are turned out to face the world with their self-confidence based, not on the belief that men are members one of another, but on the consciousness of having attended exclusive schools open only to the children of parents above a certain income level. We ought to make it clear that there is no form of excellence in the public school, whether intellectual, physical or spiritual that cannot be realised in a community school[1] attended by

1 The first time the phrase was used? (HAR)

members of all classes. We should point out that the non-local character of the public school, and its divorce from the local community, is a fundamental weakness.

An interesting footnote to this attack on the public schools comes in a letter he wrote in 1935 to his friend Russell Scott, who, leaving the service of the Cambridgeshire Education Authority became a schoolmaster in 1926 and later Headmaster of Cranbrook. Scott had sent to Morris a notice of an appeal which his school was launching for a scholarship fund. Here is part of Morris's reply:

I wish you could put your hand to a bigger thing; the re-foundation of Cranbrook, but *please* not on ordinary public school lines. You must endeavour to be spared from speeding along the tramlines of your great nineteenth-century predecessors. Our great need is for the elaboration of a communal system of education – and we should as a nation be pouring all our genius and vitality into this project. Do not make Cranbrook a respectable, antique conventional reproduction . . . Cranbrook should be something unique in the communal educational system of Kent – tho' independent. I am glad I am in the State system – there we need development and the future is with it. . . . I hope you will before long land a rich benefactor. [He added a postscript] Have we not got enough public schools – especially of the betwixt and between kind, supported by the suburbs?

ADMINISTRATORS AND TEACHERS

Beyond the problem of the public schools there remained two threats to the growth of the ideal system he had expounded; one was the danger that the main control of the system would be 'administrative and not cultural', and the second was the appalling but explicable inadequacy of most teachers. The administrators, he claimed (and he included the inspectorate), are unable to 'create and inform true education; they can ensure efficiency (an important commodity but achieved by ants and bees) but they cannot create and sustain authentic sanctions'. He categorised the administrators as hewers of wood and drawers of water; the proper architects of education were, in his view, the philosophers, artists, scientists, prophets and scholars, operating in freedom. Ideally among these last would be found the teachers. But

school teaching as at present envisaged, and school teachers as at present trained, have very little to give the majority of boys and girls between the ages of 14 and 16. The province has simply not been mapped out.

After inadequate education and training, many teachers are sent to the schools and there they remain, many forgotten for years, some for a lifetime. Some, it is true go on Refresher Courses, but we have neglected to devise for teachers a system for their cultural sustenance and continued training . . . throughout the whole of their working careers. . . . We cannot allow the existing state of affairs to continue after the war. As a result of it no class is more intellectually leaderless than the teachers.

While his curriculum reforms foreshadowed the Newsom Report *Half Our Future* (1963), the solution he proposed for the reform of teacher education foreshadowed the McNair Report of 1945 which pointed the way for teacher training for the next twenty-five years.

We have somehow to find a method of ensuring that the education and technical training of teachers goes on throughout their careers. . . . We have to examine the possibility of linking up all the schools in an area to the regional university and its education department. We could place the educational welfare of the schools and the cultural and technical guidance of the teachers in the regional care of the Universities . . . leaving the administration and administrative control in the hands of the Local and Central Authorities.

In his insistence on the permanent education of teachers through regular in-service training, Morris foreshadowed the James Report of 1972: 'Teacher training would not end at twenty-one or twenty-two; it would be regarded as a permanent process going on throughout a teacher's career.'

The suggestions for the education of the average child, or for the continuing education of teachers, stand out as forerunners of recommendations which were to be made later in various official reports; other papers which Morris produced during the war contain embryonic ideas for a whole family of reforms connected with the curriculum and public examinations. These were to come to life and grow strong in the 1950s and '60s.

Although such reforms as have come about are evidence of some progress, Morris would have been far from satisfied by what has so far been accomplished.

The pedagogic fallacy still pervades the secondary schools and, in the absence of any real attack on the in-service education of teachers, it remains rampant in colleges and departments of education. The extra year at school, starting in 1973, far from being regarded by the mass of teachers or children as an opportunity for expansion and delight, has all too often been looked upon by some with dread, and by others, prepared to accept it, as a chance to increase the number of 'paper qualifications' which can be 'worked for'; it could well become, in some areas, the 'gigantic and disappointing failure' which Morris warned about in 1942.

The various suggestions and warnings which he produced for the drafting committee of the Orange Book were almost unrecognisably muted when the slim, 30-page pamphlet appeared, badly printed and pompously written, in the spring of 1942 [25]. His recommendation that it should be written in athletic English, that it should 'create' public opinion through arousing the interest and enthusiasm of the large Penguin-reading public, had been completely ignored. Barren conversations with the Board of Education were all the fruit it bore, and the only public reaction provoked by the Orange Book were some highly satirical donnish verses in the *Cambridge Review* of May 1942, which made fun of its platitudinous and turgid style. It certainly caused no stir. Morris was mildly bitter about it, and according to his friend W. J. Deacon (Chief Education Officer of Somerset at the time), took great delight in the verses in the *Cambridge Review*.

Why were his advice and his suggestions so patently disregarded? Sir Philip Morris (who was on the subcommittee preparing the Orange Book) gives a hint of the reason; he recalled, in December 1971, the vigorous objections which Henry Morris evidently voiced when the Orange Book was published:

His real objection was characteristic of him. He thought that the Association of Directors of Education should talk about education with a warm human glow and not be preoccupied with administrative and legislative organisation and structure. His great 'fault' – a useful one – was to be so absorbed by and with his emotional thinking that he was oblivious to, and a lot of the time unconscious of, other people and their often necessarily different approach.[1]

And Sir Graham Savage, Chief Education Officer of the LCC at the time of the publication of the Orange Book, confirmed this reaction:

I should rather doubt if Henry Morris' ideas were incorporated at all strongly in the Orange Book. He was usually so extravagant in his fantasies that both matter and style would need toning down if it was hoped that the matter would carry weight. He could never get off his hobby horse and he rode it to death. I recall one occasion when he launched into a long discourse on the need for beauty in architecture and the environment generally, when he seemed seriously to consider a future when we should all be garbed in togas![1]

These observations, both from men of goodwill, devoted to education surely reveal an almost unbridgeable gap in understanding.

1 Letter to the author.

If the document emanating from the Association of Directors of Education was passed over almost unnoticed, the same cannot be said of Morris. In the Birthday Honours List of 1942 he was awarded a CBE 'for services to Education'; many thought this was a first step on the road to a knighthood, which he would surely have accepted. In March 1943, Evan Durbin, a junior minister, asked if he might visit the village colleges. He was obviously impressed for, in writing to thank Morris, he mentioned that he intended to arrange for Clement Attlee, who was then deputy prime minister, to do a tour of the colleges later during the parliamentary recess. It looked as though someone in Whitehall was speaking up for him but there may have been countervoices; Attleee did not come to Cambridgeshire.

In the summer of 1943 there was a debate in the House of Commons on educational reconstruction; in the course of this Sir Harold Webbe, member for the Abbey Division of Westminster, spoke glowingly of the village colleges in general, and of Impington in particular: 'Here, until petrol rationing stopped it, every evening during the year hundreds of youths and maidens, with their fathers and mothers, yes and their grandfathers and grandmothers, met for social and recreational enjoyment.' Kenneth Lindsay (Kilmarnock) followed him and pointed out to the House that the village colleges had come into existence 'not because the Cambridgeshire Authority wished to have them, but because one man, Henry Morris, had had an inspiration'. Chuter Ede, parliamentary secretary at the Board of Education, winding up the debate for the government, was less enthusiastic about Cambridgeshire and said: 'With regard to the Impington experiment, that is one that need not be slavishly followed.' Here perhaps is further evidence of a dampening influence, even perhaps a hostile one, inside the Board of Education.

Among politicians, however, R. A. Butler[1] was undoubtedly the most influential and consistent supporter of Henry Morris. He was to make generous tributes to him during the postwar years. Already in

---

1 Minister of Education, 1941–45. Later Lord Butler of Saffron Walden.

the early 1930s he was one of the first ministers to notice that something very important was happening at Sawston; later he used to visit Impington informally and once gave prizes away there; he spoke at the Linton Village College Students' Festival in 1948; he opened Bassingbourn in 1954 and Gamlingay in 1965.

When Bassingbourn was officially opened on 29 October 1954, Morris was on the point of retiring. Butler, then Chancellor of the Exchequer, used the occasion of the opening to pay Henry Morris a gracious but resounding compliment:

I would in many ways rather have behind me the sort of educational record that Mr Morris has than the dreadful toil and trouble of the life I lead. Speaking seriously to you, Mr Morris, I should feel that I had satisfied my ambition in my life if I had left behind so much educational achievement as you have done.

I went to visit the Sawston College shortly after the Prince of Wales opened it.[1] . . . We met Mr Morris and I am quite certain that my experience on that occasion made a profound impression on my mind when I came to plan the Education Act of 1944,[2] and I therefore feel I am coming back to pay a small debt of gratitude for the inspiration given me . . . by the planning of a college which, I believe, is at the basis of proper modern secondary education.

I should like to take this opportunity officially of congratulating the Cambridgeshire Authority on this experiment. It is not always supported. I have had many a wrangle about it (and I will tell you this in secret), when I was President of the Board of Education. . . . But one thing is certain . . . and that is that this sort of experiment is absolutely inevitable if we are to meet the obligations under the Education Act, and not duplicate effort at a time when effort and money are very precious.

Later in the speech Butler re-emphasised the way the idea of the village college combined expediency and idealism, and in his closing words, while hinting again at the hostility in high quarters which Morris had had to face, recognised and warmly welcomed the idealism which had brought success. 'If there is an excess of idealism in this experiment, which some feel, let us be thankful for it. Do not grudge the idealism – "For the spirit born to bless
       Lives but in its own excess".'

In February 1960 some of Morris's friends asked Butler to use his influence to secure a suitable honour for him before he died; but although Butler did propose him for 'consideration for a high honour', he received no further recognition from his country. This comparative lack of recognition by the government after the award

---

1 At the time (1930) he was Secretary of State for India.
2 In 1948, speaking at the Linton Students' Festival he had made the same point when, referring to that early visit to Sawston, he said: 'I decided that if we were going to reform English education it would have to be done on the lines of the Cambridgeshire village colleges. My visit definitely did have its effect on me in framing the 1944 Education Act.'

of the CBE bit deep. It was not altogether a joke when, on learning in 1946 that Philip Morris had been knighted, he remarked: 'They got the wrong Morris.'

But bitterness was not natural to him and in the summer of 1947 he was delighted to be asked to join the Education Advisory Committee of the RAF. In the following December, in the course of a bitterly cold weekend spent visiting Royal Air Force Stations, he contracted pneumonia for the first time. For someone who, until then, had hardly known illness, and who relished good health in himself as in others, this attack came as a great shock. Among the engagements he was forced to cancel was an invitation to dine at 10 Downing Street with the Prime Minister, Clement Attlee. This opportunity, unlike the pneumonia, did not recur.

After the war he became increasingly involved in national and international concerns, but these did not divert his attention from Cambridgeshire. Before the end of the war he was constructing in his mind the completed network of twelve village colleges to cover the whole of the county. In the summer of 1945 this scheme was approved by the County Council and in 1947 incorporated in the county's Development Plan and accepted by the Ministry of Education.

Typically, while dealing with larger issues, he continued to be concerned with the details of what went on in the village colleges and in the schools. His enthusiasm for the arts caused him to make a special appointment to the county staff which gave Cambridgeshire a start over most other counties in what he called 'the production and consumption of art'. Nan Youngman was an artist and art teacher, a pupil of Marian Richardson. She had been evacuated during the war to the neighbouring Huntingdonshire, and had organised courses for art teachers in Cambridge. Morris had been very impressed. Not without difficulty (because it would cost money) he persuaded his committee to create for her a new post as art adviser. She encouraged teachers to let children enjoy painting in gay colours on big expanses of paper. Like Morris she was convinced of the overriding importance of hanging original works of art, rather than reproductions, in schools. She therefore initiated a scheme for buying pictures by living artists which were then lent to schools. Soon other counties were imitating the Cambridgeshire loan scheme. Leicestershire in particular, being a wealthier county, developed it on a much bigger scale. An impressive exhibition of the Leicestershire pictures was held at the Whitechapel Art Gallery in January 1968. In the preface to the catalogue, Stewart Mason, the Chief Education Officer of Leicestershire (who had previously been an HMI in East Anglia) generously acknowledged his debt to Cambridgeshire, and 'to that remarkable man' Henry Morris.

There was a small Cambridgeshire school Mason enjoyed visiting

where the Headmistress used to encourage the children to paint anything they fancied on large sheets of paper. This was a very rare thing in those days . . . I came to the conclusion that the liberating effect of the art was having a profound influence in the school as a whole and that those schools which placed value on the arts and encouraged individual initiative were almost invariably those where you would find interesting and original work going on in academic subjects.

Under Mason, Leicestershire became well known, not only for its plan, and for its valuable collection of works of art, but for the importance accorded to art teaching, and to the experience of art, in all its schools.

Morris's reliance on Nan Youngman is nicely illustrated by the following anecdote. The war was over and he was visiting a small Primary School, where he found the whole atmosphere particularly faded and drear. 'You need colour,' he said to the head teacher, 'get off on a holiday to Italy, and when you come back go and see Nan Youngman.'

Morris took a childlike delight in holidays, especially holidays abroad. He looked forward to them eagerly and back on them with nostalgia. They gave him what he called 'psycho-physical regeneration'. He never went alone; usually he offered to help, at least by paying fares, any student or young couple he invited to join him. Companionship was all important; he needed to share his delight, share the experience of natural beauty, and of art. Food, drink and sunshine should be enjoyed with friends. And conversation was essential.

There was a tragic undertone to this eagerness about holidays. Like the passing seasons, which he noted and noticed more than most people, holidays, piling up one after the other, made him increasingly aware of 'Time's winged chariot'. When he was urging Fenn, in 1934, to join him in Italy, after describing the delights of the Yugoslav coast he added: 'You must tell your boss it's the chance of a lifetime, now while you are young.' When it seemed that the projected trip might have to be cancelled he could not accept the disappointment: 'I'm not certain that we should abandon the Italian holiday. The years are slipping by. One cannot travel in the grave. And what is money for??? We shall go to Italy in any case, and I shall provide the cash. When we are old we shall congratulate ourselves.'

He took holidays like some people take a cure. In the first months of 1937 he suffered from a prolonged cold and he wrote to me:

We must go to Florence; I must see some Art and beauty, especially Architecture . . . straight to Florence for the Easter weekend; Giotto, Fra Angelico, Chianti, food, light, colour, beauty, love. My mouth waters; then, after four or five days, to Spezia for the night. Italian naval station with a beautiful bay and Ligurian Alps for background. And then Rapallo

Florence and environs
Spezia . . . . !
Rapallo. . . . .!!
Enchanting

I am at last well and could seduce a lamp post![1]

---

[1] See footnote on page 63 for the reality of that holiday.

After the war his appetite for foreign excursions grew sharper. He took holidays almost with a sense of urgency, as though his time was getting short; took them in Rome, Provence, Florence, Spain, Austria, Denmark, North Africa. He had normally taken only one foreign holiday a year, now he seemed almost to be trying to get extra rations by taking two, and sometimes slipping in a third by going to Rome or North Africa or Sicily for Christmas. Letters to friends proposing holidays dwell optimistically on the prospect of joys to come, and scribbled postcards from all over Europe comment on immediate delights.

In 1950 he planned to go on a motor tour. He wrote to John West-Taylor, inviting him to act as his chauffeur. West-Taylor had got to know Morris when at Cambridge after the war, and was then Secretary of the York Academic Trust.

I am determined to have a first rate holiday this year and it is indeed essential. We could go by car through France, (having a careful look at Roman France) and then over the Pyrenees into Spain, keeping to the coast because of the bathing. Or we could go to Austria and visit Salzburg for the Musical Festival. . . . We could have a holiday that you could remember for life.

In April 1952, a postcard from Ischia reads: 'It has all been very beautiful and healing.'[1]

From Castello in August 1954: 'Such sunshine and glory and magical swimming *and* so much else.'

He did not always react with delight. In the summer of 1952 he tried Ireland and did not like it:

The central seedy bog through which the train goes from Dublin to Galway is chokingly dull and discouraging. Our place was in Connemara. Bare mountains, cold lakes, no trees and no concession to the senses. I did not think much of the food and disliked the roaring, unsympathetic and hostile Atlantic. No architecture . . . I never saw so many donkeys, so many cows, so many sheep, all eating and excreting simultaneously.

He didn't go to Ireland again.

In 1956 he was tempted by Denmark: 'I shall go to Copenhagen for Easter. There are works of art there – food, wine, freedom. I feel as if I could lift the roof off a whole city.' But the Danish reality proved sour. On a postcard from Copenhagen he wrote: 'I'm glad the Latin Normans conquered Saxon England and made us part of Latin and Hellenic Europe.' And in a later letter: 'I'm just back from Denmark where it rained without ceasing. Once one has been injected with the Latin and Greek genius, Scandinavia appears empty. Goethe shuddered at the thought of it.'

1 This, and other quotations in this chapter are taken from letters or postcards to various friends.

In February 1958 when he was in his seventieth year, in writing to a friend he hoped would accompany him, his longing for Italy became almost ecstatic:

I long deeply – beyond expression – to feel the Italian sun, to experience Italian beauty, Italian atmosphere, Italian bathing, Italian architecture and landscape – and Italian love! Thus one could be restored, at present I feel half dead. Could you not claim leave? Surely you could . . . Life is so short: opportunities are so rare.

He was far from being an easy travelling companion. In 1946 he decided to take a holiday in Switzerland and invited Mervyn Palmer and his wife to go with him. Palmer had been his assistant at Shire Hall. He later became Chief Education Officer at Hastings. He was to make the travel arrangements. He has described a not untypical incident:

At the critical moment the French staged a railway strike and so I booked via Ostende and Basle. . . . The trains were in an appalling state, a matter about which Henry grumbled virtually the whole way to Basle, putting the blame on me for such a stupid decision. On arrival at Basle the French side of the station reflected in every way the characteristics of the journey just completed. I found myself in a queue for the customs with our own and Henry's suitcases. He did not put in an appearance, but fortunately the customs officer was in a good mood and let us go through. The scene on the Swiss side was like a pantomime transformation. Everything was spotlessly clean, there were areas roped off with trees in small tubs and inside the roped off areas there were gaily coloured tables and chairs. Henry was already seated at one such table under a blossoming tree, with a large bottle of wine in front of him. As I appeared, staggering under the load of his suitcases and ours, he made one of those large welcoming gestures and called out: 'Oh Mervyn, do hurry!'

He managed somehow to create memorable situations, often awkward, sometimes funny. Having no foreign language, he would happily address officials and waiters in loud English. I remember the station master at Pisa being astonished on being run to ground in his office, where Henry banged with his walking stick on the counter in time to his staccato complaint that the train to Spezia had been allowed to leave before the train from Florence had got in. And once in an albergo in southern Italy, he and three friends stopped for lunch. He asked the *padrone* for 'Insalada verde'. He was delighted when she said it was available; but when the bowl appeared, containing, not the expected lettuce, but grass and dandelion leaves soused in olive oil, he turned to the proud *padrone* with the comment: 'Madam, I am quite prepared to admire your countryside, but please don't expect me to eat it.'

It was not only bad weather and unfulfilled hopes that marred some of these holidays. Sometimes he and his companions did not get on, and either by agreement, or acrimoniously, would return to England by different routes. But however disaster-laden the experience, he would allow the compensations to shine through in retrospect, and look forward with intense delight to the next time, forecasting to intended companions, 'memorable episodes', 'unforgettable occasions', 'a transfigurating time', 'inestimable sunshine and sensual realities'. He obviously got added delight from weaving sentences to express his high expectations. In the winter of 1956 he was planning a holiday in Spain and North Africa with John West-Taylor, and at the end of a prosaic letter from Cambridge about immediate engagements he wrote: 'The sun shone today and it was warmer – a delicious experience. I thought I could hear the faint strains of silver trumpets calling from the south of Spain.' Twenty-two years earlier he had written to Charles Fenn: 'I long to see Italy again: Figs, pomegranates, chianti, endless colour, the finest art, blue lakes in which one can swim for an hour on end and never get out they are so warm. In the evening the Mediterranean is magical and the moon shines across from North Africa. Bliss it is there to be alive.'

For Morris holidays afforded a kind of bliss, and a kind of transfiguration.

ARCHITECTURE, THE MISTRESS ART

Morris repeatedly emphasised the overriding importance of architecture as a means of satisfying the aesthetic, social and educational appetites of civilised man. His original concern for architecture was so deeply influence by one book, Geoffrey Scott's *Architecture of Humanism* (1914), that it might be useful to draw attention to some of Scott's ideas. As a proponent of humanism Scott favoured the classical, Renaissance and Georgian models, which he saw as being related to human proportions, and humane values; and rejected the primitive and chaotic magic of the Gothic and romantic styles. From this bias he argued that a human being, when looking at a building, identified himself with that building, and thus 'we transcribe architecture in terms of ourselves'. In at least two ways his humanism was platonic; first in his belief in the ability of man to construct, in the world as it is, a pattern of the world as it might be; and secondly in his conviction that taste and good visual manners are developed through habituation rather than through direct teaching.

Scott was appalled by the building chaos of the nineteenth century, and felt that those who had grown up before it began were fortunate:

Their eyes were habituated to an architecture of a relatively uniform intent. Our eyes have to search for it in a welter of commercial and municipal monstrosities. It is as though one had to tune a violin in the midst of a railway accident. ... The heritage of humanist architecture is being allowed to disappear ... and our Government, which finds doles for the maintenance of museums and other cemeteries, is proceeding merrily to reimburse itself by the destruction of Regent Street [42].

Morris was in total sympathy with Scott's humanism, with his theory regarding the necessity for architecture to relate to a human scale, with his platonic idealism and with his predilection for the classical as against the Gothic. This theoretical basis for his taste and for his aesthetic philosophy was evident in his own rooms in Trinity Street as well as in the neogeorgian buildings of Sawston; incidentally he agreed with Scott also about Bloomfield's Regent Street, and once commented memorably on it to a friend as they walked along from

Piccadilly Circus: 'It might have been carelessly excreted by some prehistoric monster in a moment of sadness.'

The power of architecture to promote humane values was closely related in Morris's mind to the educational influence of fine architecture, both to form taste and to induct those who moved amongst it into a state of civilised well-being. He proclaimed in a speech given at the RIBA in May 1956: 'Here let me state a belief which arises out of a lifetime spent in public education . . . that architecture is part of the essence of education' [23].

The public character of architecture underlined its importance; not only was architecture inescapable, but its influence, especially on the young, was often unconscious; hence as he said at the RIBA, it could be our 'most subtle form of aesthetic education'. But, he felt, it was essential for every educated person to be brought to an awareness of architecture. Having claimed it as 'part of the essence of education', he recommended therefore that it should be accepted as a subject for study by people of all ages. Furthermore, he insisted that it should share an equal place, being equally formative, with the study of English language and literature.

Beside the need for architecture to be developed as a subject for general study, he stressed the necessity for an extension of the whole concept of architecture. In his report on his West African mission (which he undertook in 1947, at the request of the Colonial Office – and which is referred to on page 109) he elaborated this idea of the extension of architecture:

The problem of design is really one of architecture, and architecture conceived, not narrowly, but as the ordering of the whole of our visual environment. The design of fabrics, of all kinds of furniture, of crockery and other articles in common daily use should not be tackled in isolation, but as part of design as a whole, which includes architecture. There is nothing new in this. . . . In renaissance Italy, architects like Michaelangelo carried out internal decorations and designed fabrics and garments and furniture. It was characteristic of the magnificent architectural tradition of the eighteenth century, of which only one example, that of the Adam brothers, need be quoted. The remarkable development of fabrics, furniture and household utensils of high aesthetic quality in common use, both those done by hand and mass-produced, has taken place in Finland and Sweden as a part of architecture. . . . One of the best examples of the realisation of design as including architecture, furniture, textiles etc., has been furnished by Professor Walter Gropius in the Bauhaus at Weimar, which influenced the whole of design in Germany between the wars.

The ordering of the whole of our visual environment . . . also includes the planning of the town and countryside, as well as painting, sculpture and craftsmanship. The separation of design for articles of common use from architecture; the separation of architecture from town and country planning; the separation of the painter and the sculptor from architecture, and the consequent over-development of the easel picture and 'boudoir' sculpture: all these are a contemporary development and are responsible for . . . the aesthetic failure of the modern world [17].

Naturally he linked this extended concept of architecture with the extension of that concept of education, which he had been advocating since the start of his career. But he was at pains to point out that if education and architecture were to work in harness there was no order of precedence:

Competent teachers and beautiful buildings are of equal importance; to this proposition I will admit no qualification whatever . . . it is the eternal lesson of Oxford and Cambridge. . . . Habituation is the golden method, as old as Plato's republic. . . . The school, the technical college, the community centre which is not a work of art is . . . an educational failure [14].

The alliance between architecture and education was a necessary bulwark against the cultural calamity which he long feared would overtake us. He had referred to this in his article of March 1926; in the *New Ideals Quarterly* and again in 1936 when he spoke to the Education Section of the British Association at Blackpool, warning his audience of 'the menace of aimless leisure amidst economic security, and of the decadence and disillusion and weariness that will arise with widespread intellectual and emotional unemployment' [5].

To the RIBA in 1945 and again in 1956, he repeated the same cataclysmic warnings, often using the same phrases:

We are in the presence of a vast cultural breakdown, and nowhere is this more evident than in the collapse of our visual environment. Ugliness is one of our modern diseases. We live, without complaint, in a wasteland of un-art. The evil consequences are profound. Much of the malaise of modern life is due to the lack of an environment ordered by the artist and the architect [14].

Our species, in solving the problem of poverty and overwork, is in fact moving forward to a more perilous stage in its history . . . Universal comfort with wealth and repletion, and with large margins of free time, is the next great problem of homo sapiens. The human house will indeed be swept and garnished for a fresh fate. Words cannot do justice to the urgency and wisdom of thinking out now new institutions to enable communities to face this new situation [23].

He was convinced that one means of nullifying the impending threat was for the architect and the educationist to come together in order to plan and to build new towns (or rebuild the old ones), primarily as civilising agents. In 1945 he was in no position himself to develop the building of towns, but for twenty years he had been well placed to 'order the visual environment' in which young people especially would grow up. And in his Cambridgeshire 'demonstration area', he had proved the point he had made in 1924:

The provision of public buildings for the system of public education will, in the present century, be the chiefest way in which architecture can influence the body politic . . . If the Village College is a true and workable

conception . . . a standard may be set and a great tradition may be begun . . .
and in course of time a new series of worthy public buildings will stand side
by side with the parish churches of the countryside [2].

He was not afraid to enter the professional enclosure and lecture
the architects on what they should do, not only to save themselves but
to save humanity:

One of the main functions of architecture in high civilisation has been to
give significance to man's physical environment, either in terms of feeling,
through awe and the numinous . . . or in terms of the human body and its
manifold physical states. . . . Modern architects have to search and experiment to find out how far the structural possibilities of modern materials
are capable of performing externally this humane, sensuous and aesthetic
function [23].

He also stressed that the architect should not only aspire to be a
designer of buildings, but should also learn to work as the member of
a team which might include other artists and craftsmen: sculptors,
painters, potters, landscapists. At the same time he must enlist the
professional planner. Here, as always, Morris was careful to point out
that by planning he did not mean merely the locating of roads, sewers
and buildings. The planner needed to take into account the cultural,
social and economic life of the community with a view to giving
maximum encouragement to civilised living. 'One main means to this
end is to group our local communities round their colleges and
secondary schools' [23].

The community college for secondary and for adult education
would have its theatre, reading room, library, its laboratories, common
rooms, games facilities and dining rooms. It would be the focal point
of the new towns. In the suburbs, the secondary school and the
college of further education would form the nucleus of the community centre.

He pointed to the positive advantages, educational and economic,
to be gained from this coordination of educational buildings. But he
was not so far in the clouds as to think that all the amenities provided
could be shared by all the users of all ages. He recognised that some of
the rooms, perhaps a whole wing, or even one building in a complex,
should be 'sacred to the grown ups', and decorated accordingly; for
example the lecture rooms could be 'panelled with sycamore or walnut plywood and furnished with easy chairs'. Every city, every
suburb or country town would have its community centre, providing
at all stages for the family group in the same way as, in the past,
the parish church served the family from birth to death.

By bringing together what he called the intellectual, the corporate
and recreative needs of a community, he was, he felt, reflecting the
ideal aimed at by Oxford and Cambridge, and by extending this, we
would redeem the daily life of every local community. But in the
Oxford and Cambridge of his day he saw no flicker of recognition

of the overriding importance of architecture either from dons or students. He deplored this in an address he gave in 1957 to the Council of Visual Education: 'Visual illiteracy amongst our highly educated classes is an astonishing phenomenon. People of great taste in literature and music, mathematicians and scientists with a sense of order and truth are frequently . . . aesthetically stone blind' [24].

He went on to underline the illogicality of the new university of Keele, which had been founded with a view to achieving a humane education by bridging the gap between the arts and sciences, but Keele was doing nothing to ensure that students were offered one of the most essential elements of a humane education: the opportunity to grow up among works of architectural merit in a landscape of beauty. 'God help Keele!' he exclaimed.

If university teachers in the matter of visual insensitivity were past hope, he could hardly expect more from school teachers; but he deplored the lack of leadership in this matter given by the teachers' associations. He quoted with scorn a teacher representative, who, at a meeting on the postwar school building programme had said: 'Mr Chairman, I trust no *aesthetic* considerations will stand in the way of school buildings being put up rapidly after the war.'

But while he castigated users and architects' clients (including chief education officers), and cited their insensitivity as a reason for pressing for architecture to be a subject of general study in schools, he blamed still more the architects themselves. Not only had they done little to educate their clients, they had failed, except in a few outstanding cases, to perform what he termed architecture's 'external service' to the local community. He was dismayed too by the architects' abdication from public responsibility, in that the best students emerging from the schools of architecture (often encouraged by their teachers), turned their backs on employment with a public authority where they might be faced with socially important and challenging work; instead, they sought jobs in private practice, designing villas and swimming pools for rich customers.

The need for architects to experiment with new materials, to learn to work in a team with other artists and craftsmen, and to look upon themselves as co-workers inside the current technological system (rather than holding themselves apart from it), all these ideas he shared with, or derived from, Gropius and the Bauhaus.

While it was valuable and important for such ideas to be expressed generally in England, the special ideas which Morris himself put forward to architects and educationists are more striking, and have possibly been more influential. The first of these sprang from the example he gave when he persuaded Gropius to design Impington. While he wanted and encouraged good young British artists to enter public service (and liked to remind them that Christopher Wren was an official architect), he realised that the existing system of local authority architects did nothing to encourage innovation.

Since the building of schools was the chief occupation of local government architects, it was essential, if school building was to be improved, for outside architects of national and international fame to be encouraged to build some of our local schools. He put it this way:

At the present moment the largest part of the architectural intelligence of England is not able to make its contribution to education because of the somewhat rigid system of official architects. Some way must be found round this obstacle. During the next ten years an enormous programme of building for colleges and schools will be carried out. . . . We want the help of outside architects, not only because of the technical and artistic contribution they would make, but because of the sheer weight of work to be done. This is a problem about which the RIBA, all the Teachers' Associations, and Local Government bodies should get together at once under the aegis perhaps of the Ministry of Education [14].

Arising from this suggestion regarding the employment of distinguished outside architects, and immediately connected with it, was an administrative proposal, the formation of an independent architectural development group inside the Ministry, in place of the existing arrangement, whereby one or two architects were employed to vet plans submitted to the Minister. Not only was this proposal eventually to be adopted but the functions of the group, which he sketched out in this speech, were to a great extent included in the eventual structure of the future Architects and Buildings Branch in the Ministry of Education. Following on the general suggestion quoted above, he continued:

The time has surely come when the Minister of Education[1] (who understands and is a friend of the arts), should reconceive the function of his architectural department. It should be made far more influential. It should be increased in numbers and should be reinforced by the recruitment of some of the best of our younger architects. Acting on the assumption that well designed buildings and furniture and good interior decoration are a necessity and not merely desirable, the department should aim at nothing less than giving a definite and imaginative lead on the aesthetic aspects of all educational buildings. And this it should do with the avowed aim of lifting the standard of taste of the whole community.

Do not let us be put off by suggestions that this programme would be expensive and what is called 'idealistic' and 'visionary'. It is eminently practicable. . . . We must underline what is a fact, that well designed and beautiful school buildings can be built at a reasonable cost, and that gay and exhilarating colours do not cost more than County Council Brown or Municipal Green.

A second task is still to be done; it has to do with the technical aspect of school buildings and their efficiency as a working tool of education. This is the scientific and quantitative aspect of school buildings. . . . It includes on the one hand, materials, lighting, storage, orientation, heating, corridors,

1 At this time, R. A. Butler

equipment, styles of tables, desks, seats, etc. etc., and, on the other, the fundamental problem of the organisation of the school, that is, the relationship of the various rooms . . . to each other.

We sorely need an authentic corpus of sifted information and experience about the equipment and organisation of school buildings (as well as a bibliography of work that has already been done . . .) having in mind, of course, the pupil and the experience of teachers. Such a body of detail can only be brought together by the central ministry working with some instrument of permanent consultation between teachers, inspectors, administrators, architects and manufacturers [14].

The Architects and Buildings Branch of the Ministry was not in fact formed until 1949. It quickly proved highly influential in raising the standards of school building throughout the country. The prime mover behind its formation was Antony Part (now Sir Antony Part), at that time a young civil servant in the Ministry of Education. He was not in fact aware of the paper by Morris, quoted above. The idea came to him as a result of his increasing conviction that a merger of the architects and administrators in the Ministry was long overdue. He became the first administrative head of the new branch, and Stirrat Johnson-Marshall (now Sir Stirrat Johnson-Marshall), who had been in the county architect's department at Hertford, and who already knew Morris, became the architect head. Morris may not have had anything directly to do with the setting up of the Architects and Buildings Branch but he certainly approved of it, and early in 1949 was in touch with Part and Johnson-Marshall with a view to using the services of the branch for the benefit of Cambridgeshire.

Already at a meeting of the Education Committee on 14 December 1948 he had obtained approval in principle for the building of a new regional college of further education in Cambridge. This was an ambitious concept which would combine the aims and virtues of Gropius's Bauhaus with the community functions of the village college. At the same meeting the committee had also agreed that the services of a full-time architect should be engaged to prepare an architectural brief for the new college. Morris may well have felt that if he could get the newly formed A and B Branch to prepare the brief it might be all the easier, later, to obtain final agreement for the college from the Ministry. At the same time it might prove correspondingly difficult for his own committee to back down. But if this was his plan, it failed.

He invited Johnson-Marshall and Part to come to Cambridge early in 1949 to discuss with his committee exactly how they should set about the task. They arrived at Shire Hall expecting to be given an important commission for their newly formed department, to draw up a brief and perhaps eventually to design a fitting building for this revolutionary new departure in further education. But for once, Morris had failed to prepare the ground in advance. Soon after the meeting began it became clear that the committee were in no way prepared to let the Ministry have a hand in designing 'their' college.

There was no way of bridging the gap, and Johnson-Marshall and Part left Cambridge that day in no doubt at all that the Architects and Buildings Branch was not immediately going to be able to experiment in Cambridgeshire.

A CAMBRIDGESHIRE BAUHAUS?

Failure to get the Regional College of Further Education designed by the A and B Branch did not deter Morris from attempting to realise his ambitious plan by other means. Although the councillors had curtly dismissed the Men from the Ministry, it seems that they were not totally opposed to using an outsider, at least in the initial stages. In March 1949 they agreed to the appointment of Jack Howe, an independent architect from London, to prepare an architectural brief for the new college; Howe was not a complete stranger to them as he had worked as chief assistant to Maxwell Fry during the building of Impington.

Since the college was to be something entirely new in educational architecture, Howe visited Sweden, Denmark, France and Switzerland in July 1949 in order to look at their latest technical schools and colleges and to consult with architects. By the end of the year he had produced the brief [36], a carefully composed document which was historic. For a building put up by a local authority a brief of such complexity was at that time unheard of, but the proposed building had to be unique if it was to match Morris's bold and original concept. In thirty pages, packed with descriptions, drawings, charts and tables, Howe forecast the detailed requirements which would transform Morris's dream into a reality of concrete and steel, bricks and glass, lawns, trees and flower beds. Flexibility was vital, and therefore Howe recommended a method of construction which would enable the size and the use of spaces to be altered without excessive expenditure of time or money. In 1949 this was still a new approach which had been pioneered by Johnson-Marshall in the postwar Hertfordshire schools.

A magnificent new site of 48 acres on the Trumpington Road had been earmarked since 1947 for the building which might replace the already overcrowded Cambridgeshire Technical College and School of Art, and at the same time accommodate the projected county college which was expected to take students between sixteen and eighteen years old on day release as soon as the 1944 Education Act was fully implemented. The new college, when completed, would offer facilities until then unheard of in further education, both in the type and variety of courses offered and in the opportunities which were to be provided for recreation, refreshment and even for residence, since students would come to it from far afield. It would develop into a kind of community polytechnic and justify the name which Morris intended for it: The Cambridgeshire Regional College of Technology and Design.

Side by side with the traditional departments of science and engineering, business studies and institutional management, a Humanities Faculty would be established, including departments of music and foreign languages. In addition an entirely new faculty would be created, the School of Design. This would have its own accommodation, including an experimental workshop; this faculty would offer courses in the fine arts, ceramics, sculpture, printing, industrial design including furniture design. These courses would be open to students of all departments, since the aim would be to create new relationships between design, craftsmanship and industry. The Building and Architecture department would be another important element within the School. Full-time three year courses in architecture would be offered, and would include town and county planning, civil engineering and landscape design. In this way it was hoped to open up new perspectives for architects, while drawing the attention of artists and craftsmen to the supreme importance of architecture.

A touch of pure Bauhaus philosophy is seen in a report to the Governing Body of the Technical College which appears in the Minutes of the Education Committee of 14 December 1948. It must have been written by Morris.

The aim of the School of Design would be to deal with design in all its forms, in fabrics and furniture, crockery and other articles. . . . Thus the design of things in daily common use would not be tackled in isolation, but as part of design as a whole, which includes architecture. One object of such a School would be to meet a widespread need for artist-designers who can design prototypes for mass production by the machine of things in daily common use. The machine has to be accepted, the essential thing is to see that the prototypes are designed by competent designers who have had the necessary training.

The recreational opportunities at the new college were generous and civilised. Two restaurants were included in the plan, one large and one small. Specific recommendations for these reflect Morris's concern for detail and for a proper environment for taking meals:

Every effort should be made to avoid the canteen atmosphere. This can be helped by the use of colour, window curtains, and sympathetic illuminations. On no account should fluorescent lighting be used. Generous windows should be provided with access to an external terrace which may be used for open air meals in summer [36].

The auditorium of the college had to be designed not only for public performances of plays, opera, concerts and for films, but also for use as a music and theatre workshop. In addition to the two gymnasia, a swimming bath would be included, not simply because swimming was important as a branch of physical education, but because, as the brief thoughtfully states: 'It is attractive to watch and will provide a centre of movement and interest.' The bath was therefore to be built in a central position, near the main promenade, which might form a raised gallery along one side of the swimming bath. The stress on the importance of visual impact runs like a refrain through the brief; a consultant landscape designer was to be appointed at an early stage so that the site could be adapted suitably and according to a previously conceived campaign of planting. Finally, and regarded as essential, original works of art (pictures, pieces of sculpture, and at least one large mural) would be included in the building.

When the brief was almost complete Howe went with Morris to see Part and Johnson-Marshall at the A and B Branch, no doubt to get their blessing. Strangely enough Howe was given no hint at the time of the previous intention for the Branch to design the college. Possibly this concealment can be attributed to collective embarrassment. Morris himself was delighted with Howe's work, and looked forward eagerly to the time when their building should start. The brief was presented to the Technical College Subcommittee on 17 January 1950. It was welcomed and the committee recommended that the RIBA be asked to nominate four possible architects for their consideration, and that the names of the County Architect and of Jack Howe be added to the list. One of these six would be selected to prepare detailed plans for the college.

But then ominous signals of economy cuts began to come from the Ministry, and the County Council felt obliged to ask the Chief Education Officer to 'report on the extent to which the needs of Further Education could be met by building additions on the existing site [of the old Technical College].[1] The Technical College Subcommittee fought back. They resisted the suggestion that additional building on the cramped site of the existing college could ever provide a satisfactory solution to the problem and they recommended that: 'The Authority's project for building on a new site, already approved in principle by the Minister of Education should be proceeded with.'

But they lost the battle. Hundreds of thousands of pounds have since been spent on buying up land and in fitting new buildings into the small and unsuitable area round the old technical college. It is sad to think that if the Russians had launched Sputnik five years earlier than they did, the tidal wave of technical college building which followed that launching, might have swept the Cambridgeshire Regional College of Technology and Design on to that still empty and magnificent site on the Trumpington Road.

1 Minutes of the meeting of the Technical College and School of Art Subcommittee, 16 May 1950.
2 *Ibid.*, 3 October 1950.

Morris had failed. He knew it and blamed himself. His vision of a great and unique community polytechnic withered away. Nor was this the only one of his postwar plans and recommendations which was to fall on stony ground. When after the war he moved out into wider and unfamiliar fields he seemed to loose that sureness of touch which he used to show when operating on his home ground. The network of village colleges in Cambridgeshire was successfully extended, but his other postwar projects and educational excursions outside the county seemed often to contain some fatal flaw. Some of his friends and former disciples were perhaps among the first to notice a falling off. Robert Logan, an early admirer from his under-graduate days, in the early 1920s, who became Chief Education Officer of Worcestershire during the war, and who acknowledged a huge debt to him, has written sadly of this postwar period:

The ideas, the vocabulary, the habits of assertion that had been so bright and wholly acceptable were perhaps fading. . . . Henry's unpredictable timing, his exaggerations, his disconcerting silences, so much of the apparatus that was acceptable in the elder brother playing host grew less tolerable and even galling. . . . That Henry was never (outside his own efficient office and his own tiny court) professionally popular with the mass of his fellow workers was to be expected. But what might have rung true enough during his pioneering days was becoming less convincing.

Logan once asked him to define good administration and he had replied: 'I don't know, but it is close to irritability.' This may have worked at Shire Hall, but in Whitehall with top civil servants, or with colleagues working in local government, his facility for exacerbating his equals or even his superiors did his causes no good. He refused to toady, would never assiduously cultivate a relationship with potentially helpful officials. And he was consistently scornful of those who failed to see golden possibilities with his own perfectionist eyes. Thus, in the ventures described in the following pages, although his aims and ideals were still of the highest, success was often blocked simply because his characteristic qualities made his arguments seem unconvincing to those with power. This does not alter the validity of many of his contentions; often only today can we begin to see what he was getting at and that they contained the seeds of ideas which later have been accepted and have flourished.

Before the concept of the new technical college began to take root in his mind he was offered two opportunities to exert an influence in areas where he felt he was fitted to make a lasting and positive contribution. In the event his contributions were modest, but the formulation of ideas and ideals resulting from these tasks is of more than passing interest. Both the invitations came from Whitehall, neither from the Ministry of Education. At the end of 1946 the Colonial Office asked him to go to West Africa for two months to conduct a one man enquiry and report back. At about the same time he received an invitation from Lewis Silkin (later Lord Silkin), Minister of Town and Country Planning, to join him on a part-time basis, and advise him on the social aspects and implications of the New Towns, some of which, like Harlow and Hemel Hempstead, had already been started.

AFRICAN ADVISER

The invitation from the Colonial Office defined the scope of the enquiry fairly narrowly: he was asked to visit the West African Institute of Industries, Arts and Social Science at Accra, to look into the way this somewhat hybrid establishment was working, and to make recommendations. In particular he was asked to comment on the effectiveness of the original concept of the Institute, in which two research departments, one of technology and one of social science, were intended to cooperate with a view to promoting the humane development of modern industry in West Africa.

The institute had been set up in 1942 and had suffered from being a war baby. The needs of wartime Britain had starved it of adequate staff and distorted the original aims. It had been forced into the mundane task of producing materials of immediate use for the allied war effort, and at the same time the original idealistic aims had become clouded or even forgotten. It was these original aims, rather than the administrative departmental problems which interested Morris. He hoped that his report might eventually be instrumental in building up a model in West Africa which would point the way forward for relatively primitive societies everywhere, and lead them directly to a humane and sophisticated way of life without having to pass through the century-long industrial barbarism suffered by the West. He contemplated writing a classic report which would, he said, 'show the Colonial Office possibilities it had never dreamed of'.

He recommended separating the two departments of the Institute; each would be attached to an African University. The more important one, in his view, would be renamed and radically reformed as the Institute of Architecture, Planning and Design. It would form part of the newly founded University College of the Gold Coast at Accra. The Social Science department should, he felt, be re-established as an

Institute in the University of Ibadan in Nigeria. Although separated, the two former departments should not be divorced. He explained this by stating his belief that:

Architecture is *the* social art. The need of a deep consciousness on the part of town planners and architects, designers and technologists not only of tradition and the past but of the contemporary social forces . . . is obvious. What those social forces are in West Africa an Institute of Architecture would most likely not discover for itself without the aid of expert sociologists [17].

He therefore recommended that lines of communication between the two institutes be kept open, especially for the benefit of the architects.

When he came to the details of the proposed Institute of Architecture he recommended that the scope of its work should be exceptionally wide, and that the various departments ranging from Town Planning to Ceramics and Weaving should be informed by the concept of the fundamental unity underlying all branches of design: 'The study and the practical experience of working with materials (stone, wood, metal, clay, glass, fabrics) in various handicrafts and the study of colour are as necessary for architects as for designers of furniture and fabrics.'

The common source of these ideas and of those he developed when planning the Regional College of Technology and Design in Cambridge, is, of course, Gropius and the Bauhaus; and while the relationship between architecture, the fine arts, and craftsmanship is described most clearly in this African Report [18] it is deeply rooted in the ideas expressed in Jack Howe's architectural brief for the College, and later realised at Digswell House as described below.

During his African visit he was struck by the deterioration in taste which sets in when primitive native arts are exploited by the machine and dominated by market forces. In Accra he had visited workshops where Africans were trained to design and make furniture: 'The products are lamentable in design, they are an example and a warning of the desperate decadence that may become widespread and endemic where ancient traditions are being transformed and vulgarised by an insensitive technology.' Once again he looked to Gropius and the Bauhaus to provide a remedy, and was not ashamed to reveal the source of his advice:

In training designers it would be wise to adopt the method which Gropius employed at the Bauhaus – the dual method of training whereby the designer was taught by a craftsman-technician and by an artist-designer, working together. There was thus an organic connection between the Bauhaus and the factory, and between design and industry [17].

Another unexpected, and, as far as the Colonial Office was concerned, original recommendation in his report owed nothing to

Gropius but much to the basic doctrine which had informed the village colleges: his belief in the importance of providing a meeting ground for a wide variety of people with specialist interests. Ideally universities should provide such a meeting ground, and originally they did, but already he saw, even in Oxford and Cambridge, this ideal being forgotten, as the barriers between academic specialisms rose higher and higher. By establishing his Institute within the university at Accra he wanted to ensure that it 'should have some method of informal but nevertheless influential contacts with those who are members of and workers in other faculties . . . with administrative officers, industrialists, and those who man the professions of law, medicine and teaching'.

By this means he hoped to counter the constricting influence which specialisation, both in universities and outside, was increasingly exerting on so-called educated people. He therefore envisaged accommodation being provided at the institute for visitors who would come there either for study or for refreshment. Such visitors, whether they came for a meal or to spend a few nights in rooms provided, would perhaps begin to appreciate something of the lure and importance of architecture and the visual arts.

Finally he could not resist including in his report another of his enthusiasms: cooperative enterprise. The economic situation in West Africa lay a long way outside his brief, but this did not deter him from recommending strongly that the cooperative workshops which he visited should be extended. He saw these as a form of adult education, which needed encouragement.

Through them, education is connected with vocation and with the mastery of a particular skill through which the man or woman makes a contribution to the community. I noted the social side of the co-operatives, their meetings, their meals together. . . . If I had anything to do with the problem of popular Adult Education in West Africa, I should base it in part . . . on the co-operatives. Here is the instrument for a genuine adult education. At all levels man achieves status, both mentally and socially, as master of a single technique. . . . Reinforced by his arts, the dance and song and with his religion he is master of his environment. It is in this kind of context that an adult education with a vital relevance can be carried on [17].

The Institute in his opinion should see big, and act big. One of its first tasks should, he thought, be to design a new town for West Africa, and with it a number of new villages. These would be built to meet the advent of the unavoidable messiah, Western technology, from which so many Africans understandably expected so much; understandably because, as he aptly quoted Robert Bridges in his report: 'They have seen the electric light in the West.' No doubt the potential of new towns was already at the top of his mind as he flew back from Africa in February; almost immediately he started preparing a paper on the subject for Mr Silkin, the Minister of Town and Country Planning.

He came back to a bitterly cold Cambridge, and Africa must have seemed a long way away. He was enthusiastic about his new part-time post at the Ministry and procrastinated over the African report. It was nearly a year before it was sent off to the Colonial Office where he had once foreseen it would open up undreamed of possibilities. But he had moved far outside his brief, and to the Colonial Office mind his 'extravagant fantasies' (see p. 89) must have seemed quite unrealisable. The potential of the African Institute of Industries, Arts and Social Science had to remain unrealised.

COUNTRYMAN IN THE NEW TOWNS

In spite of his profound attachment to the countryside he had always been a 'civic' man; he knew where the civilised virtues sprang from and saw, in the planned town, the only means of extending these in the twentieth century. Not that he approved of the preachings and policies of the Garden City enthusiasts of an earlier generation. He was vitriolic about Letchworth and Welwyn, places 'for ball-less intellectuals fluting about art, with no pubs, and no genuine culture'. But in his Blackpool speech of September 1936 [5] he had said: 'Our towns are squalid and chaotic dormitories sicklied o'er with commercialised amusement. They should be, and one day they will be, deliberately organised by the community for the art of living the full life.'

By 1946, the opportunity of being closely associated with such deliberate organisation came within his grasp. David Hardman on becoming a junior minister in the Attlee government, wanted to persuade Morris to put his well tried talents and his genius to work on wider fields than Cambridgeshire. In a letter to Hardman in April 1946, replying no doubt to a proposition put forward by Hardman, he made it quite plain that there was only one job that would 'lure him away from Cambridge and educational administration' and that was a position where he would be responsible for advising the Government on all the cultural aspects of town and country planning, for he believed that 'nothing less than the planned town is required for the total education of the future'.

He felt that Britain was in an ideal position, after the war, to lead the world. A new democratic sense was evolving as a result of the war, and this could be enhanced and developed through planning our towns and cities so that they should become, themselves, educational instruments. And here he was not thinking merely in terms of aesthetic education through habituation, but social and political education.

For twenty-four years he had been concerned with schools, yet from the beginning he had proclaimed that 'the school is not enough', it needed to be set within a wider frame, within a newly conceived form of adult education in a new community setting. But even this expanded and embracing idea of the school did not satisfy him; the town itself needed to be redesigned; the dreary urban development of the interwar years convinced him all the more of this necessity.

Following the letter of April 1946 David Hardman had spoken with Lewis Silkin, the Minister of Town and Country Planning. Negotiations were protracted, and it was only in December, shortly before Morris left for his African mission, that the Education Committee received a request that they should release Morris for two days a week, to act as 'Adviser to the Minister on cultural and community aspects of the work of creating New Towns'. The committee said they were flattered and agreed to the request. 'MR SILKIN WANTS MR MORRIS' shouted a headline in the *Cambridge Daily News*. Reading this in the education offices the next day, one of the clerks was heard to respond, with some feeling: 'Mr Silkin can have Mr Morris'.

His enthusiasm for the potentialities of the New Towns was one of the great advantages he brought to the job. In addition he was supported by the Treasury, which liked the money-saving effect of the Morris doctrine of combining schools with community centres; he was fully supported also by his Minister. Mr Silkin's speech, when moving the second reading of the New Towns Bill in May 1946, suggests that he was already in accord, if indeed he was not already in touch, with Morris: 'I want to see the New Towns bright and gay with plenty of theatres, concert halls and meeting places. Our towns must be beautiful. Here is a grand chance for the revival or creation of a new architecture. . . . The New Towns can be experiments in design as well as in living.'

On the other hand, the civil servants at the Ministry of Education had never been kindly disposed towards Morris's ideas, and he still had to deal with them. Other officials, whether from Whitehall or in the New Towns, were not inclined to welcome this stranger in their midst. This was particularly true with local government officials, who must have looked with some disfavour on one of themselves coming in and advising them.

He had other disadvantages to contend with. He was not used to working as a member of the national Whitehall system, and the administrative style which had worked well in Cambridgeshire was very different from that he would have had to employ in order to succeed in this much wider and more critical field. In Cambridge when drawing up a report it did not matter if he wandered far outside his brief; in Cambridge he knew his officials and his councillors, and they knew him, and over the years they had come to accept his foibles and extravagances. In Cambridge he had a power base from which to operate; he knew his backers and could identify likely opponents.

But among the staff of the Ministry of Town and Country Planning, and in the various departments of the New Towns he knew no one, and could be sure of no one's support. To get his ideas implemented he had to rely only on his powers of persuasion. In this new situation these, unfortunately, worked as much against him as for him. J. E. McComb, who at the time was General Manager of the Welwyn

Garden City and Hatfield New Towns was, in many ways, favourably disposed towards Morris. But he saw his failings: 'He was a great talker, and consumed a tremendous amount of time, accordingly he got rather short shrift from a number of General Managers.' B. G. H. Brook Taylor, a social relations officer of Hemel Hempstead in Morris's time, has elaborated this theme:

Apart from the difficulty of his ideas, Morris had an intellectual attitude which irritated practical people. He made the mistake of wearing his intelligence too obviously. He thrust it at you with an occasional quotation, which reminded me of the days when people stressed their classical education by the use of Latin and Greek tags.

Secondly, and probably more important, his professional achievements and experience in Cambridgeshire, which had prompted Mr Silkin to select him, served in fact to discredit him in other eyes. Another General Manager, A. V. Williams of the Peterlee Development Corporation, has written: 'I admired the tenacity with which he pursued his *idée fixe*. What he achieved in Cambridge as Director of Education (*sic*) was a considerable contribution to the stimulation of village life. To have extended the idea to the new towns would, I think, have been a mistake.' And McComb, on this subject wrote: 'It seemed to me that what went well in a sparsley populated rural area did not fit into a densely populated urban area, and to be populated moreover by Cockneys.' Such quotations surely show clearly the mixture of benevolent misunderstanding and professional irritation which he encountered.

But thirdly he was impatient. As in the case of his plans for the Cambridgeshire Technical College, he sometimes failed to do his homework; abandoning the caution of his early days, he failed to reconnoitre the ground over which he intended to advance. One of his first acts, on taking up his post at the Ministry, was to issue to all the General Managers of the New Towns, an eight-page memorandum entitled 'Education, Community Centres and other Cultural Institutions'. In this he recommended a policy of grouping the buildings concerned: the schools, community centres, libraries, concert halls, colleges of further education, around one focal point. 'If one of the major features of the New Towns is to be cultural, . . . such groupings provide one of the few available opportunities of giving the modern town a significant form and atmosphere. [18A].'

The assumption that one of the major features of the New Towns was to be cultural was made without taking soundings, without finding out whether even lip-service was being paid to this ideal. Morris seems also to have assumed that his experience in Cambridgeshire and the success he had achieved with the village colleges, would give enough weight to his arguments for them to be persuasive. To give added weight he arranged for staff and managers from the Development Corporations to visit the colleges; these cortèges became a familiar feature of Impington life. But the visits seemed only to reinforce in the visitors their convictions that what had been done for the sleepy fen folk was not transferable to the energetic and commercially minded refugees from the big cities, and they returned, sometimes impressed, but not prepared to copy.

Their resistance was understandable. Some of the managers had already produced draft plans for their towns before Morris appeared on the scene, and did not like being told that these should be revised, and revised according to a theory which they did not necessarily share. A note of a discussion held in the manager's office at Hemel Hempstead New Town is typical of many *aides-memoire* which survive. It is dated 11 October 1948:

Covered various types of schools, county college and community centres. Suggestion made that Mr Morris's grouping of community centres with secondary schools on campuses was of a primarily cultural origin and that the social side would be more emphasised by placing the community centres in the neighbourhood centres. Mr Morris continued to argue his point.

A similar *aide-memoire* dated 18 January 1951 refers to a discussion at Peterlee and reads: 'Mr B. stated that it was quite out of the question for the Secondary Schools to be used by adults in the evening as this was contrary to the practice and outlook of the County Council.'

If the general managers proved difficult, the county education officers in the New Town areas were often more so. They were not going to take advice from a man few of them had heeded before the war. Many of them had a clear conception of what adult education did and should involve: examination courses and hobbies classes, and if some of them were prepared for 'dual use of facilities', or at most the addition of an adult-wing to an already planned school, then this was as far as they would go. Morris's ideal of a multidimensional complex catering for all ages and offering opportunities for recreation and study was simply indigestible.

The fact is that the New Towns owe little to Morris's influence. As Norman Fisher said in his Mellows Lecture: 'It cannot be said that Henry's advocacy of what was needed in the New Towns fell on very fertile ground. Town planning in our generation has been conceived by surveyors and adorned by architects. It has never been imaginatively developed in terms of total human needs which Henry Morris realised was essential' [34].

In Cambridgeshire, his own county, he was still not without honour; in the New Towns he was not only without honour, he was virtually without power. Brook Taylor, now Social Relations Officer of Telford New Town, and one of his more severe critics in the early days, has however written: 'To be fair, a great deal is now happening in the sort of direction in which he was pushing, although largely by people he would neither have liked nor understood.'

HILLTOP AND DIGSWELL

During his time with the New Towns Commission he had some small successes. He persuaded the Hertfordshire County Council to build the college of further education in the centre of Hemel Hempstead, rather than at the edge of the town, as originally planned, and he originated two special projects, Hilltop at Hatfield and Digswell at Welwyn, which were interesting at the time, and which remain interesting. Although Hilltop has failed to fulfil original hopes, Digswell has proved successful.

Promoters of community centres have always been exercised over the provision of alcohol; there is seldom agreement about whether or not to allow it. In their pamphlet on community centres produced in 1946, the Ministry of Education devoted several paragraphs to the problem of bars, and witnesses were called to put the case for and against [30]. The recommendation of the Ministry was predictably that 'it should be for the community concerned to decide whether they want a bar or not'. In the New Towns the Ministry recommendation was particularly unhelpful since the community was not there to consult when plans had to be made for community centres. Morris's solution was simple. In South Hatfield the centre would be built in the pub. He succeeded in getting the idea accepted, paid for and realised by two breweries, working together with the Hatfield Development Corporation. There was initial opposition and a public enquiry, but the scheme was eventually blessed by the Minister of Housing and Local Government and by the Licensing Justices. The name of the pub was significant. Rather than call it the de Haviland Arms or the South Hatfield Community Centre, it was simply called Hilltop (because it stands at the top of a hill). Besides the normal pub rooms, it contains a restaurant, a hall for meetings, several committee rooms and a welfare clinic. Guinness were persuaded to advance money to McMullens, the local brewer, to pay for the 'dry' accommodation. The Development Corporation commissioned Lionel Brett (later Lord Esher) to design the building, and the corporation played a large part in operating the scheme in the early days.

A significant aspect of the written agreement between the Development Corporation and McMullens, was that the Users' Committee of the Centre was to be responsible on three days a week for 'fostering social group work' while McMullens retained the right to use and let the social premises on the other days of each week for dinners, dances and social gatherings of a more 'commercial' character.

The original idea was Morris's, and he had been instrumental in enlisting support from Guinness; J. E. McComb, the General Manager, was eager to cooperate, and he brought in McMullens. Morris spoke with other Development Corporations about the possibility of their setting up dual purpose pubs, but at the time there was on response. Significantly, at Cwmbran New Town in Monmouthshire, 'Fairwater House' is a pub, operated on the same basis as the original

Hilltop. The General Manager of Cwmbran is J. E. McComb, who moved there from Welwyn. Under the first landlord Hilltop was used as intended; friends met in the café when out shopping; the old people's club met there weekly; the children's clinic and Sunday school classes were held regularly on the premises, and all the usual activities of local 'hobbies groups' were carried on there. Access to the bars was, for most, an attraction. Community activities were supported by a much higher proportion of men than is usual when refreshments are confined to tea and sweet biscuits. But after the first landlord was replaced cooperation waned, and Hilltop has split (like an amoeba), one wet cell run by the brewers and the other, the dry one, by the Hatfield Rural District Council.

The other experiment staged by Morris during his time with the New Towns Commission was at Digswell House, near Welwyn. This has been much more successful than Hilltop although, as with the first village college, Sawston, the early years were stormy and often tense. But successful survival after a stormy start only proves the validity of an original idea. Digswell like Sawston, survives and flourishes; and if it does not yet do all that Morris hoped, it still embodies many of his ideas and ideals. It was his final throw, and fitting that it should have been concerned with a facet of life which reflected his deepest interest: the development and coordination of the visual and plastic arts in the community, for the community.

Throughout his life, in articles and speeches, he had expressed his belief that 'the active practice and enjoyment of all the arts is as necessary to humanity as food or air'. In the New Towns therefore he felt that one of the most pressing needs was to provide opportunities for 'the production and consumption of art'. Possibly because he became convinced that contemporary man should support and be involved with contemporary art, he always held living artists in special regard. This was not confined to giving them special respect as artists but also (and particularly when they were young and unrecognised) he was concerned for their welfare, for their living and working conditions. He believed therefore that society should not only encourage but provide for the living artist. This had become even more necessary since the private patron had virtually disappeared from the scene.

His dual concern for the contemporary artist and for his art caused him to see in the New Towns a unique opportunity for the community to replace the private patron, and furnish the squares and public buildings of the town with necessary fountains, sculpture and other works of art by living artists. Those who were directly involved in building the New Towns had, he felt, more than an opportunity, they had an obligation to play the patron, and this was as important as providing drains and roads. He was agreeing here with S. Giedion, who wrote in his *Walter Gropius, Work and Teamwork* [35], that only in this way could the urbanist fulfil his moral responsibility of 'awakening in man a realisation of needs and aspirations that are at present slumbering within him'. The key part in this exercise should be played by the architect; it was for him to conceive the town in such a way that these necessities would be included in the original design, having evolved from discussions between architect and artist.

Until this time no institution had ever been set up consciously to bring the artist into direct contact with town planners, architects, manufacturers and the local public. Nor had anyone planned an institution which would offer the artist a market place and also proper accommodation for working and living in. This concern had exercised Morris during the war, when he had discussed vaguely with Jacquetta Hawkes and other friends the possibility of establishing a Laboratory City at Bettiscombe in the West Country, where it was envisaged that experiments would be set up specifically to try to solve the problem. The Laboratory City remained a dream, but from 1947 his official connection with the New Towns Commission gave him the chance he needed to realise an immediate solution on the ground. He crystallised his ideas in a paper: 'The Contemporary Artist and the Community' [22] which he wrote shortly after his appointment to the Commission: 'What we have to do is to relate the artist in a realistic way to the living community and at the same time enable the community to become acquainted with the artist, to know him and accept him as easily as they do the doctor.'

But the immediate need was for living space and studios. Because the art market was in London, artists tended to congregate there uncomfortably and expensively. 'There should be a diaspora!' he wrote. Just as Cambridgeshire had provided between the wars a demonstration area for the early growth of the village colleges, so he hoped to provide in one of the New Towns a model sanctuary for artists, which having proved itself, could be repeated all over the country.

His idea was to find a country house going cheap, not too far from a New Town, and preferably near a university, which could be easily converted to accommodate a group of artists and craftsmen. Here the residents would have individual studios and workshops; bedsitting rooms or flats would offer privacy. At the same time, the individual artist 'living in', would have the chance, whenever he felt like it, of visiting other members of the group, to talk, learn, explain or observe. An atmosphere of mutual encouragement would be generated. Since it was intended to give priority to young artists who had not yet made their name, and who were only recently out of art school, the easy availability of practical and psychological support from other artists, often of their own generation, would be especially valuable and important. The artists were to be drawn from widely differing fields. While the plastic and visual arts were to predominate, Morris hoped that poets and musicians would also be included among the residents; the word 'museum' would be reinvested with its original meaning. Here he envisaged summer festivals when the studios would be open, works of art exhibited, and concerts, recitals and readings would add richness.

In order to prevent such a community turning in on itself and shutting out the neighbourhood, twoway channels of communication would be established between the group and the surrounding district, through part-time teaching by the artists in local schools and colleges, and through regular sales and exhibitions of works of art in local galleries, and shops, as well as through the summer festivals and open days in the house itself. Firms and local authorities would be expected to commission work from the resident artists. Places for new tenants would regularly fall vacant since artists would normally only stay until they were established and able to set themselves up independently.

Morris tried first to get the General Manager of Harlow New Town to take over Kingsmoor House, south of the town, but the proposal was not greeted with immediate enthusiasm. But James McComb, who as General Manager of Hatfield and Welwyn, had already responded positively to the idea of Hilltop, welcomed this new idea and proposed Digswell House as the 'demonstration area'. This was a regency building set in a modest park between Welwyn Garden City and Welwyn; the New Town was to grow up in that area. The lease was due to expire at the end of 1956; the Development Corporation could then let it at a very small rent. A suitably constituted Digswell Arts Trust would administer Morris's scheme, and help secure commissions for the artists. Among the expected patrons were naturally the Development Corporation itself, local industry and the County Council. Looking far into the future, Morris saw the Digswell Festival of the Visual Arts, aiming 'to do for the appreciation of the contemporary arts what Glyndebourne has done for the appreciation of music'.

The reference to Glyndebourne is perhaps significant, a pointer to an aspect of Digswell which some of the artists found distasteful. Dinner jackets and evening dresses were not often, if ever, seen at Digswell, but there was an establishment aura about the members of the Arts Trust. However, money and favour had to be won somehow, so it is not surprising that the first Trustees whom Morris and McComb persuaded to back the project, included people like Lord Balniel (M.P. for Hertford), Gordon Maynard (local industrialist and Deputy Chairman of the Development Corporation), Sidney Broad (Chief Education Officer of Hertfordshire), David Hardman (Secretary of the Cassel Trust and formerly Parliamentary Secretary at the Ministry of Education), Bryan Robertson (Curator of the Whitechapel Art Gallery), Sir Gordon Russell (President of the Design and Industries Association) and Herbert Read. The quest for 'fellows' (significant title) began at the Royal College. Paul Fletcher, a former student of the college and a pupil of Epstein's, was recommended. He was the unofficial leader of a small group of sculptors who had settled around Maida Vale, and who were desperately looking for studio space. In the summer of 1956 Morris met Fletcher at Jack Pritchard's flat in Hampstead, where more than twenty years before the first auspicious meeting between Gropius and Morris had taken place. Morris and Fletcher got on well. A second meeting was arranged in the latter's flat in Warwick Avenue. Here Morris expounded his Digswell scheme to the group. It seemed to fit their needs exactly and they responded with enthusiasm; he was impressed by them. It was a memorable evening.

Digswell House still needed structural alterations, and it was not until the spring of 1957 that Fletcher and John Robson, also a sculptor, moved in as the first tenants; by the end of the year six 'fellows' of Digswell were installed. It had been agreed that Morris would act as 'administrative secretary' to the group. During the first few months all went well; not so much smoothly as intensively. Fletcher remembers long conversations with Morris lasting far into the night about art, literature, and especially about people: or extended walks with him around London, visiting Heal's furniture department and discussing contemporary design, and Morris seeking Fletcher's advice about what to buy there and never being able to make up his mind. Later there were dramatic differences of opinion between Morris and other members of the group, including Fletcher himself. He recalls being ordered in his own sitting room to remain seated while Morris strode up and down, furious because without consulting him, Fletcher had accepted a part-time teaching job in London. He also vividly remembers Alan Denley, one of the early 'fellows', normally a gentle man, and a subtle thoughtful painter, pursuing Henry down the staircase at Digswell, in anger.

The highly charged relationship between Morris and the group was, Fletcher now thinks, a measure of the greatness of Morris, and of their own miscalculation of what his long-term aims actually were. They suspected that the Digswell project looked back for sustenance and inspiration to William Morris and that they were expected to contribute to a twentieth-century version of the art and craft movement. Fletcher admits now that they were wrong, and that the Digswell project, as conceived by Morris, far from looking back,

heralds the future and that the need for people everywhere to be involved directly in creation, and particularly in art, is now much more obvious: Increasing population, gargantuan towns, finite resources seem to lead quickly to a desolate grave. I now realise that Henry saw this very clearly before many others and worked in a tangible form to do something about it. Digwell was part of this.[1]

Many of the altercations were merely petty; often because agreements between Morris and the group had been left vague. There were arguments about rent, and about the number and extent of the outside commitments that the artists might take on. Some found Morris's interruptions and repeated visits to their studios both time-consuming and irritating. John Brunsden, a print maker, who shared a studio

[1] Letter to the author.

with John Sturgess, describes the two poles between which their relations with Morris alternated.

At the beginning he was a very active man, cycling round the Garden City on his old lady's bike with a little wicker basket on the front. His twinkling eyes and gay whimsical humour, and digs at those in authority, captivated us. But later the shuffling steps along the corridor leading to our studio, confirmed by the snuffling of a continually running nose, would cause us to pray for deliverance. . . . He would come in and work up a fury against another member of the group, against one of the Trustees, or against us personally.[1]

In particular, Fletcher, as the first member of the group, felt aggrieved, since it had been understood (and he still has the letter stating it) that all members would participate in selecting new recruits, and that Fletcher, as 'acting leader' would be involved in the interviewing of candidates. In the event, this was undertaken by a subcommittee of the Trustees; members were not consulted and Fletcher was not on the subcommittee.

All these differences tended to sour the atmosphere; Morris became forgetful and unreliable. But he was a sick man, and these first 'fellows' failed fully to realise this at the time, or to make allowances. Later, as Morris's condition clearly deteriorated, the Fletcher group dispersed and new 'fellows' took a softer line: Graham Arnold, a painter who joined Digswell in the summer of 1959, remembers him differently.

Morris always became extremely anxious about distinguished visitors to Digswell, especially if there was a chance that they might contribute to the Trust. He would come to Digswell to discuss details with Arnold:

Shuffling up and down my studio, hat on and muffler round his neck, he would momentarily forget the purpose of his visit, and not minding that I carried on painting, begin one of those marvellous discourses touching on all kinds of subjects – maybe Constable and landscape, or the similarity between Keats and Mozart (a favourite subject), or the need for good fresh food and so on.

As the time for the visit approached, Henry's nervous excitement would become almost uncontrollable, but at the hour we would be waiting in the main hall at Digswell, for the visitor. Introductions over, a tour of the studios would begin, at a pace reminiscent of an early 1920 comedy film. On one occasion, Henry was showing an important visitor the studios when to my surprise he appeared alone at my studio door so exhausted that he was hardly able to speak; he simply murmured: '*Homestead Court*'.[2] We got into my car and left immediately.[3]

Graham Arnold also recalls one of the most successful of the 'extramural' aspects of Digswell, with which he was closely connected;

1 Letter to the author.
2 The residential hotel in Welwyn Garden City to which he had moved in 1958.

this was the education programme, by which arrangements were made for parties of local people to visit Digswell, talk with the members and see their studios. Each visiting party was given an introductory talk, a well prepared exposition of the aims and ideals of Digswell. Morris attached much importance to these overtures and before he fell really ill he liked to conduct them; he used to call it 'spreading the word'. Many local Workers' Educational Association groups came, and also parties from the Women's Institutes, the Townswomen's Guilds and from neighbouring art societies. At one point these visits became so frequent that the artists complained that they were being interrupted too often, and a system of rationing had to be imposed. This, however, shows the pressure there was for the outside world to get to know the artists and their work. The visits continued, often from the same groups on a regular annual basis, as there were always new productions and new artists to see and to learn from.

Recruitment in the early years was largely organised by Morris. This always involved an interview in a London hotel with a sub-committee of the Trustees. They fired questions and viewed the candidate's work. These occasions were often felt by the artists to be embarrassing, especially since they had usually already visited Digswell, when Morris had shown them round, and probably decided their fate. Most of the recruits were young and little known to the public, but several distinguished artists and craftsmen were also invited to come to live and work at Digswell. Some had special needs which the Trust tried to meet, and from which others following them could also benefit. Ralph Brown stayed for five years, and while there executed the figures for the fountain at Hatfield New Town. Hans Coper, already established as a potter, joined in 1959 and stayed for six years. He was induced to come partly by the prospect of working as a design consultant, with architects and heavy clay manufacturers, carrying out experiments and research in ceramics and other materials. Subsequently he had the satisfaction of seeing many of the prototypes which he had made at Digswell going into mass production as tiles and cladding for prefabricated buildings. The Maidenhead Brick and Tile Company gave him £1000 to build a special kiln to his own specifications. The Building Research Station at Watford approached him with the problem of how to make external panels of reinforced concrete look attractive, and he became involved in CLASP (Consortium for Local Authorities Special Programme) which produced prefabricated units for building schools. In his studios in the stables connected to the house, Coper also made the six giant candlesticks for Spence's Coventry Cathedral. The stained glass windows of the nave of Coventry were made by Keith New in his high studio in the former drawing room of Digswell, where the previously blocked-up north window had been exposed to receive the huge wooden frame in which the glass was assembled.

Donald Brook's acceptance of a place at Digswell was the occasion for building of a special cedarwood studio costing £700. For this Morris persuaded the Noel Buxton Trust to contribute half, while his friend Ian Phillips, now a Trustee, gave the rest. Peter Collingwood, the weaver, made various requests to the Trustees before he agreed in 1958 to come to Digswell, including the provision of extra windows in his studio, to give more light. He recalls that he did not get all he had asked for and that Morris upbraided him for not being more demanding and then proceeded himself to pay for glass panels being fixed in the door of the studio, which increased the light considerably. Collingwood admits that originally he went to Digswell entirely for material reasons; he had no capital and he needed a special place in which to work, and a cheap flat. But he became convinced that the benefits he gained during his stay were by no means all material. While still there he confirmed the validity of many of Morris's aspirations for Digswell. First, there was the advantage 'of living and working among a group of people who share one's basic assumption that what one does is important', and, secondly, there was the advantage of seeing how other artists worked and learning from them, using their expertise even in humdrum domestic ways and experiencing the delight of genuine community cooperation.

There are experts in stone, clay, metals, wood, fibres, synthetic materials, paper, paint, dyes, glazes etc. If ever anything breaks or if one wants to make some new bit of apparatus, the person with the appropriate knowledge and tools is always at hand – and always very willing to help. This is taken for granted here, but I think it will be sorely missed by most people when they leave [26].

By the beginning of 1959 there were fifteen artists in residence. Peter Collingwood's account gives an idea of the range of craftsmen and artists represented; etchers, letterers and print-makers were also included. Writing to a friend in 1959, Morris said: 'Digswell is now full with a veritable constellation of young artists and craftsmen and I believe something remarkable might happen.'

When the time came for the official opening, he must have felt, as with Sawston, that he had once more given his blood; his energies had been drained almost dry in the course of implementing one of his most cherished ideas. He had striven successfully and achieved the unlikely cooperation of a widely disparate crew: civil servants, councillors, industrialists, aristocrats, academics and probably most difficult of all, artists. He had not only shown his diplomatic and administrative skill, he had become, once again, a beggar: the Elmhirsts, the Noel Buxton Trust, the Cassel Trust, Ian Phillips, many of the old names which had supported Sawston with money figure again.

It was a fine day for the opening in May 1959. Lady Mountbatten performed the ceremony. The artists put on a special show for the occasion. They too were present. 'Aren't you proud of them?' Lady

Mountbatten asked him. 'Fairly,' he replied, rather pointedly. He had not emerged unscathed from the struggle.

Digswell might be (indeed has been) regarded by some as the figment of a failing imagination; the kind of dotty House of the Arts which Angus Wilson might have dreamed up as the setting for a novel. But this would be quite wrong. Morris, throughout his life, had sought a solution to the problem of accommodating the artist in an industrial society. With William Morris, Ruskin, and many others, he recognised that the industrial revolution placed gigantic constraints on artists and craftsmen driving them into a cosy or uncomfortable and often lonely confinement. To lift these constraints, and to reintroduce the artist to society, and society to the artist, it was no use rejecting the new products of the age, no use trying to ignore the technical revolution, and it was self destructive for the artist to seek refuge in flight. The isolation of the artist meant the paralysis of inspiration.

Art needed to come to terms with science, and the artist needed to come to terms with the machine. In the paper already mentioned, 'The Contemporary Artists and the Community' [22] he wrote: 'Mass production by the machine is a technique which must be accepted by man as piece of good fortune. But on one condition: the prototype of the articles that are mass produced must be designed by artists.' At the same time, the artist needed to break out of his confinement, to associate first with other artists working in other fields, and also with the community; this was necessary not only for the health of the artist, but for the health of the community too. Digswell House offered this dual opportunity, and still does so.

Digswell has not yet been reproduced, but this does not invalidate the experiment. There is no lack of candidates for the vacancies which regularly occur, and already more than fifty artists have passed through and been affected, some profoundly, by its atmosphere and unique quality. Moreover Digswell has given them an assisted takeoff into their eventual careers which is powered, not from an outside source, not from the influential Trustees nor from the ghost of Henry Morris, but from their own peers and companions whom they have coincided with at Digswell. This is what Morris wanted.

The problem of the artist in contemporary society will not be solved in any one way, but the Digswell scheme points to one. It had been tried and proved practicable. It could still be a prototype for a whole network of similar centres.

13 DECLINE

The frustrations of his postwar world so far described were all part of his professional life. But in the 1950s, private and domestic worries also plagued him. True, they were offset by occasional expressions of official appreciation of his achievements, and by recurring moments of delight afforded by Cambridge, by healing holidays abroad, and by continuous contact with friends. But in spite of friends and devoted attention, he became more and more lonely. One feels now that the deep insecurity which he must always have felt, and which he hid so well for most of his life finally in his last years broke through the strong barriers he had erected against it, weakened as he was by illness and the weariness of age.

Illness, which he had always detested and done his best to fend off or ignore, forced him into hospitals and nursing homes. The first attack of pneumonia came in 1946 but it returned in the middle fifties at shorter and shorter intervals, along with pleurisy and, in the last years, arteriosclerosis which intermittently affected his movements and his memory. He tried at first to ignore these lapses from his habitual state of fitness, and refused to believe that there was any chronic infection lodged in his body. 'For your private ear,' he wrote to a friend in 1954, 'I've not been at all well lately, owing, I think, to the nervous strain of retiring. I went to the nursing home for two days continuous sleep.'

By retiring altogether from his Cambridgeshire post at the end of 1954 he thought he might be able to devote himself more fully and effectively to the New Towns; but the extra time merely involved him in more wearisome travel and further fruitless and frustrating meetings. A new cause for distress overtook him in 1956. He had already, in 1945, been forced to move his home when Lady Darwin wanted to re-occupy the *Old Granary*, which she had leased to him when he moved from *Trinity Street*, in 1938. Now Peterhouse wanted the house in Fitzwilliam Street, where he had established himself comfortably. This was serious, for his home was very much an extension of himself. And not only did he have to go househunting, but he had had to hunt also for housekeepers. In fact, ever since his faithful and understanding housekeeper, Miss Godfrey, who had been with him since the early 'thirties, retired in 1944 a stream of widows and elderly spinsters had tried to fill her place. None lasted. There were intervals when he kept house for himself, which he quite enjoyed. 'The truth is,' he said once to his secretary Mrs Bimrose, 'I myself am a better housekeeper than all these damned women.'

He failed to find another house in Cambridge, and took a flat for six months in the Lawn Road Flats in Hampstead; there Molly and Jack Pritchard could provide him with company, for they lived on the top floor. But he was no Londoner. In June 1957 he was writing: 'This lovely weather, strangely enough has been a trial in London to me, so used to lying on the grass in the university bathing sheds and swimming in the Cam and idling in the evening in the green shades of the garden of Peterhouse, or with candle light in the garden of 15 Fitzwilliam Street.'

He was homesick; and for any of the three successive homes he had made in Cambridge, homesick for his own furniture, his pictures his fabrics and rugs from which emanated a common and familiar gaiety and a peculiar elegance. He was homesick too for Cambridge itself, for the buildings and gardens and the river. This attachment went far back; in a very early letter of August 1921 he had written: 'Such lovely weather . . . the Backs are breathlessly beautiful and the buildings muffled in silence . . . hardly a sound, occasionally an American looking up at a window thro' his pince-nez.' And still in March 1956 the attachment held: 'I confess that the inner part of Cambridge is very beautiful, and has a mildness and crisp glory which is missing in other cities.'

After London, he moved at the end of the summer for a few months to a Victorian house in Hurstpierpoint, Sussex, where he became a neighbour of David Hardman's. Finally in 1958 he moved to Homestead Court, Welwyn Garden City. But these places for him were little more than addresses, he felt at home in none of them. Most of his furniture had had to be stored when he left Cambridge and most of it stayed in store, so never again was he able to recapture the visual and spiritual delight of his Cambridge homes.

However the events surrounding his retirement in December 1954, after thirty years as Chief Education Office of Cambridgeshire were triumphant. In November Bassingbourn, the first village college to be completed since Impington, was opened by R. A. Butler, at that time Chancellor of the Exchequer. The generous compliment which he paid Morris on that occasion (quoted on p. 91), he capped with the words: 'I hope when you retire, Mr Morris, you will continue to help in the world of education with your idealism and your imagination.' Norman Fisher, by then Chief Education Officer of Manchester, wrote a long and generous farewell article in *Education* [32]. There were the usual presentations and official speeches. Thirty of his close friends and professional allies invited him to be their guest at a private dinner in the newly opened Wordsworth Room at St John's. He was obviously moved, and, in a very short speech, expressed his gratitude.

This, when he remembered to do it, was something he was good at. It was at this time, 1954, that he wrote one of his most touching and most revealing letters, to Molly and Jack Pritchard:

I have been thinking a great deal of what I owe to people. The debt is a big one. But I have no doubt that I owe more to you than to any other two people. The reason is quite clear. You gave me confidence, more than anybody, and consistently. Jack, more than any one man believed in me and made it clear, without display. . . . You Molly did the same for me.

The benefit in confidence and security for me over thirty-four years has been unstatable. I knew I could, without hesitation turn up at any time at Lawn Road and be welcome – welcome is not a good enough word. I mean received with affection so that one felt one mattered, (a lovely feeling). Neither of you, by the way, ever made demands. I also had the subconscious assurance that if difficulties or dangers arose which I could not cope with I could if necessary go to you without an apology on my lips.

Well I have told you the truth, and it is good to do so.

Another gesture of public recognition came to him at this time and appropriately enough it was to the Pritchards to whom he first broke the news in confidence of his impending election as an Associate of the RIBA. 'I cannot resist telling you,' he wrote 'since I know it will give you pleasure, that the RIBA have written to say that the Council propose to elect me as an Honorary ARIBA. . . . There is nothing I could have liked better.'

During his last years he was often asked to speak in public, but he almost always refused, often inconveniently at the last moment. L. G. Stewart, the Music Adviser in Cambridgeshire, remembers vividly driving him one morning from Cambridge to Welwyn Garden City where he was to speak at a teachers' meeting. Half way there Morris turned to Stewart and said: 'Look here, I'm feeling very nervous, you'll have to read my speech for me.' Stewart said he couldn't possibly do that. When they reached the hall, Morris sat on the platform, and after he had been introduced by the chairman of the meeting, he stayed sitting down, told the audience that he was not feeling well, and took his speech from his pocket and asked the chairman to read it. This the chairman did, and the speech was applauded. Morris stood up to acknowledge the applause, and proceeded to give another speech lasting half an hour! After that, said Stewart, he was perfectly all right.

He was repeatedly asked to broadcast, but usually refused. He agreed, in February 1955, to talk after the 9 o'clock news about the village colleges, but wrote to a friend that he found the talk terribly difficult to compose: 'I'm so stale on the subject.' The script, in fact is still fresh, and gives a succinct account of his ideas of the Village College [21]. The RIBA gave a dinner to Walter Gropius in April 1956, at which he was one of the chief speakers, and his last important public appearance was before an audience of architects on 15 May 1958 [23].

His last move in 1958 to Homestead Court, the residential hotel in Welwyn Garden City, was not a happy one. He had two small rooms and no view, but he wanted to be near Digswell. Illness dogged him. He was persuaded at the end of 1960 to write his letter of resignation to Dame Evelyn Sharp, then Permanent Secretary of the Ministry of Town and Country Planning. He hated doing this, and insisted on including a phrase, where he expressed the hope that he might still be of service 'in a voluntary capacity'.

Throughout this time at Welwyn Garden City he was devotedly attended by Dorothy Bimrose, who had been his secretary at Cambridge since 1943 and had moved with him as secretary to the Digswell Arts Trust. She visited him every day, often cooked meals for him, and when he became forgetful saw to it that he took his pills in the right order and at the right time. Old friends visited him. In March 1961 he was moved to a large hospital near St Albans, and put into a geriatric ward. Friends frequently visited but most of the time he seemed hardly to know what was going on. He had, however, lucid moments when his old liveliness burst out and sometimes his old enthusiasms; once he telephoned David Hardman from his bed and asked him to recite, 'that Housman poem'. Hardman responded:

> Loveliest of trees, the cherry now
> Is hung with bloom along the bough,
> And stands about the woodland ride
> Wearing white for Eastertide.
>
> Now, of my threescore years and ten,
> Twenty will not come again,
> And take from seventy springs a score,
> It only leaves me fifty more.
>
> And since to look at things in bloom
> Fifty springs are little room,
> About the woodlands I will go
> To see the cherry hung with snow.

Graham Arnold, who took over responsibility for the education programme at Digswell, got to know him well during his last years and has written of him with great sympathy:

I first met Henry Morris one gloriously sunny day in July 1958 at Digswell House. We strolled in the garden and I listened to the story of Digswell and the plans for its future. It was while I was discussing these problems with him that I happened to mention the opening line of 'The Prelude': 'Oh there is blessing in this gentle breeze'. The response I received at this was electric. I remember that moment vividly and from it our friendship began.

Towards the end of the summer of 1959 I came to live at Digswell House. It was soon after this that Henry was seriously ill. He made a partial recovery and I began to visit him, in the evenings, at his flat at Homestead Court. By Christmas of that year our friendship had developed a pattern which remained unaltered until his death in December 1961.

Almost every evening I was at Digswell, which was usually four or five times a week, I would see Henry at 6 o'clock at Homestead Court. We would stroll across to the Hotel for a drink and sometimes dinner, and spend the remainder of the evening either in the lounge of the Hotel, in the flat, or driving in my car to some place of interest not too far away. I would leave Henry in his flat between nine and ten o'clock. Frequently our meetings would have to take place at the hospitals at St Albans or Hill End, and would be restricted to normal visiting hours. At Cambridge, when Henry went to a Nursing Home after a stay in hospital, it was possible to go for a drive in the evenings.

Being a witness to the day by day deterioration of Henry's powers made it possible for me to understand his thoughts and arguments where others, who may perhaps not have seen him for several weeks or so, would be helpless at being unable to make any intellectual contact with him, particularly if they knew Henry well before the onset of his first illness. Those who were close to Henry during this time were aware that what was most precious for him was calmness. The freedom from any unforeseen event was, however, impossible. If any unforeseen event did occur, during periods when Henry was calm and when the immediate past and future had a set pattern of regularity, it would disrupt his mental state with terrible abruptness and with a marked deterioration in his health. It might be weeks before the fine balance was again restored. Very often a phone call from a friend who had not seen Henry for some time would be enough to undo weeks of slow recovery.

Henry would occasionally wish to go to Hilltop at Hatfield. He was intensely curious to discover at first hand whether or not it was proving the successful social amenity he had hoped it would be. We would begin by entering the lounge of Hilltop and having bought a drink, and never disclosing his identity, Henry would approach people in the lounge and ask them if they liked the building or if they felt it was really used, or if they thought it was a success. Most of those approached were exceedingly wary and said little; occasionally however, one or two would talk freely about Hilltop and Henry would cross-question them for a considerable time. Having spent an hour or so in the lounge we would move into the Public Bar. A small group of friends would be playing darts and a number of people were usually sitting at tables. Again we would obtain drinks and begin asking questions. Once we were asked to leave by the publican after Henry had unsuccessfully been trying to engage a group of earnest dart players in conversation. We left with a chuckle and entered the hall near the lounge. A group of teenagers were rehearsing a play, and, unseen by them, we quietly sat in the semi-darkness and listened for a short time. Henry only said 'good, good'. He was thrilled to find that Hilltop was being used and that it was playing an important part in the cultural and social life of Hatfield.

During Easter 1960 we planned a trip of a week or so to Cambridge. Henry was keen that I should complete a series of etchings of the various Colleges, and he was eager to show me the exact spot he wished them to be seen from. He also wanted to show me King's College Chapel which I did not know. We arrived at Cambridge about midday. After a brief lunch we walked across to King's College Chapel. We went inside, and sat down. Henry did not say a word. We remained sitting for about twenty minutes then Henry suddenly rose and walked slowly out. We came straight home, after collecting our bags from the hotel, and Henry never mentioned King's College Chapel again.

That summer of 1960 seemed to have an unlimited number of fine tranquil evenings and we would often drive out into the nearby country-side, perhaps towards St Albans or Hertford, and, stopping the car in a quiet lane, we would walk a few yards and stand listening to the leaves moving in the trees overhead. There was one particular stretch of field with a stream meandering across lined with willow trees, behind which rose a small rounded hill where cattle would be grazing. This meadow seemed to Henry to contain the essence of the English countryside, and we returned to it on countless evenings. Its beauty was almost more than he could bear. As we approached this field and glimpsed the cattle grazing, he would lift his hand and say 'Look, the cattle are still in the meadow'. One luminous still evening, while we were visiting this field, he told me how before the first World War he had sat in an orchard with friends, on such an evening, and how they had talked of eternity. He had thought then that his life was like eternity, and that the quality of that single evening would last for ever. The war had come, and he had never seen his friends again. He paused and said to me 'Death has the smell of new mown hay'.

During those two years there were times when Henry was so near to death that it seemed impossible that he could ever recover. Somehow he did recover, and what was even more remarkable was that the pattern of our meetings continued unchanged. Although these appalling periods were frequent, what I remember most vividly is of evening after evening when we would sit talking as the sun set. We would watch the sky undergoing the most wonderful colour changes until eventually it sank into a blue blackness. We talked mostly about poetry. It seemed to me that far from reducing Henry's perception and consciousness, his illness had produced a state of heightened awareness of those poets he had known and loved. The know-ledge of his own certain death meant that suddenly he saw poetry which he believed he knew well in a new way, as if suddenly he had discovered a new level of consciousness. He would attempt to explain this enlightenment and the way this affected the poets he admired above all others – Wordsworth, Keats, Arnold, Meredith, Tennyson and T. S. Eliot. This subject was terribly important to him; it was a reassessment of what his life had been and of what had meant most to him. I know how much these poets did mean to him, and how much his thinking was concerned with their work during this period. The ultimate truth, which I could not fully grasp, was that enlightenment, so dearly gained, resulted only in a tragic despair.

Henry knew he was a dying man. Death was always near at hand, having an almost visible presence. He continually believed that there were three of us, but having been persuaded that we were together, he would refer to the passage in 'The Waste Land' –

> 'Who is the third
> Walking beside you?
> When I count there is only you and I
> Who is the third?'

Towards the end, but before the final collapse, it became impossible to leave Homestead Court. We would walk across to the Hotel, but even that small distance was utterly exhausting. We continued, however, with our meetings. The last walk, of any length, was one cold starlight night in late

May. Henry had seen the cherry trees from the Hotel lounge windows and suggested that we might walk to them on our return to his flat – a distance in all of about one hundred yards. That journey took an age. Henry was so frail, his feet were dragged along the ground, and he had to hold on to me for support . . . We reached the cherry trees . . . petals showered down upon us like snowflakes.

On 10 December 1961 Henry Morris died and the funeral service was held four days later. It was a moving but also a strangely joyful occasion. David Hardman and Norman Fisher spoke briefly. There were moments of laughter. David Hardman reminded that congregation of friends:

On such occasions as this he would vehemently warn against pomposity; indeed he often said he would bring down fire and brimstone and treacle on anyone who tried to make his funeral an important rhetorical occasion. Then he would smilingly add: 'But you won't forget a few things I needn't mention, will you?'

This book has mentioned many of these things. If there are doubts as to whether they are worth mentioning, the next chapter should dispel them. In it the current development of Morris's ideas and achievements is catalogued and traced back through people who knew him, or worked with him in Cambridgeshire during his lifetime.

14 MORRIS IN THE 'SEVENTIES

The community school came to this country in three distinct waves. Between the wars, the serious crisis in rural education (referred to by *The Times Education Supplement* in 1924, and quoted on p. 22) was met by Henry Morris in Cambridgeshire. Here he created the village college in order to enrich and invigorate the rural region, and make it attractive enough in itself to withstand the pull of the town. The second wave appeared after the war. The Butler Education Act of 1944 had postulated county colleges, where compulsory part-time education would be provided till the age of eighteen, for all who were not attending school full time. As Butler foresaw, the village college offered a useful model for these, since the proposed county college could conveniently and economically be grafted on to an existing secondary school, provided that the school was specially equipped and designed to welcome and accommodate adults. The postwar development plans submitted by several county councils (e.g. Devon and Somerset) referred specifically to the village college as the example that would be followed; other counties (e.g. Leicestershire), adopting the same strategy, acknowledged the connection with Cambridgeshire while changing the name from village to community college. The obligation to provide county colleges was never pressed by the government, but some local authorities went ahead with their plans to give young people and adults the chance to spend their leisure in community schools inside which the secondary school was also housed. Others merely tacked an adult wing or a youth centre on to a secondary school, where classes or youth club activities could take place.

In the 1970s we are witnessing the third wave, the third period of growth. This has brought the community school into the centre of cities. The impulse behind this came from the 1967 Plowden Report [27]. This floated the idea of Educational Priority Areas, where poor housing, poor schools and poor families were seen as requiring compensation. The report encouraged teachers in these twilight areas to try to get parents to involve themselves in the school and in the education of their children. For teachers this was an unfamiliar and sometimes even an unpopular suggestion. In the past they had tended to look on parents in such areas as being either hostile or indifferent to the school, while they saw schools as outposts of enlightenment in a dark and uncivilised neighbourhood. The Plowden doctrine did not entirely dispel this last opinion, but suggested that teachers should adopt a missionary spirit, not only towards their pupils but towards the parents too, aiming to convert them to the ways of the teachers' world. This was a part of compensatory education.

Further thought and more recent investigations have caused a shift in this avuncular doctrine, and schools are now encouraged to welcome and accept the community and the parents as they are. In the words of Jerome Bruner: 'The deprived mother needs to eb involved not compensated.'[1] So we arrive at the point where the problems of the inner city schools are seen as social and economic as well as educational problems, and the neighbourhood as playing a positive and potentially useful part in its own education. We are in sight of Morris's educational community, and of getting rid of what he called the insulated school; we are moving away from the world where education is confined to infants and adolescents, and where teachers tend to become 'pundits and tyrants'. We are also proving his contention made in 1924 that: 'The village college would not outlive its function, for it would not be committed to any intellectual or social dogma' [2].

Cambridgeshire, with Morris's village colleges, had a start of at least twenty-five years over other local authorities, so it is not surprising that the development there of community education, looked at from an administrative point of view, is nearly complete. The original plan, sketched out by Morris in the 1924 *Memorandum*, has now been realised. A network of twelve village colleges covers the county. They are all schools for people over eleven, some of them comprehensive, each one set in a community centre, and providing opportunities for education and recreation for anyone, of any age in the area. Morris himself insisted that the village college could be one of our freest institutions, and it is therefore interesting to note that in Cambridgeshire, the colleges have developed in some ways which might have surprised him; and they are still developing.

Credit for carrying out the Morris plan in full must go chiefly to George Edwards, formerly Warden of Bottisham, whom Morris persuaded to become his assistant in 1944. He succeeded as Chief Education Officer in 1954. The ideal set up by Morris is available to all the colleges; some get closer to it than others. None, of course, achieves it totally.

Echoes of battles long ago can still be heard:

I consider that Henry Morris quite cold-bloodedly set out to destroy the influence of the church in village life. . . . The measure of Henry Morris's success can be seen in the dead and dying villages of our country (*sic*), and the atheistic spirit which largely pervades them. I wonder if Morris and his successors at Shire Hall are pleased with this monument.

1 *The Times Educational Supplement* 27 October 1972.

This letter, with its interesting suggestion that Morris lives on, appeared in the *Cambridge Daily News* of 4 March 1972. It was signed by John Hornsby, Rector of Stretham, Ely. Replies came quickly to defend Morris and to point out, with examples and evidence, the increase in social, educational and good-neighbourly activities which the college had made possible, and which had not existed before.

David Farnell, in his 'Henry Morris. An architect of education' [32] confirms this, and many others working in the colleges today are enthusiastic about the advantages they bring. Staff talk about their easy relations with parents, and parents about the easy relations with staff; there is a lack of tension between the evening and the daytime activities, so often a feature of 'dual purpose' schools where the head of the school relinquishes his headship each evening to the head of the evening institute. Staff emphasise how educational activities can go on side by side, and often in conjunction with recreation, and that the college is acceptable, and regarded as suitable, for the most unlikely events. One college expects to have a wedding reception for former pupils almost every Saturday. At another mothers leave their children in the crèche run by older pupils, while they themselves join the sixth-form humanities course. In one college the pensioners come in during the day to play billiards and dominoes, and then keep an eye on their grandchildren as they read the daily papers in the library.

An interesting development in Cambridgeshire is the recent foundation of the Ely Federation of Village Colleges under a single governing body. This coordination makes possible the efficient pooling of resources beyond the capacity of a single college. Thus the four colleges contribute to the six-form centre, which forms a part of the City of Ely College – one of the Federation. Other concentrations can be expected in other colleges. Transport is organised by a fleet of buses and minibuses belonging to the Federation.

George Edwards is confident that the whole concept will surely earn Morris's approval when he returns (as he used to threaten to do) 'to take his terrestrial leave' in Cambridgeshire.

But Morris's relatively obvious solution to the problem of schooling, adult education and community recreation, almost got pinned down behind the county boundaries of Cambridgeshire. One explanation for this might be called the Innovation Time Lag, the process by which new ideas about education are often locked away for at least a generation, and then are suddenly rediscovered and presented to the world, often in a new language. The community schools, community colleges and neighbourhood centres which are springing up today in widely different parts of the country bear a distinct resemblance to Morris's village colleges. It is not important to prove consanguinity, but their conception can very often be traced to Morris.

There is a good human and political explanation for the Innovation Time Lag, and the case of Morris and the colleges illustrates it well. Innovators are often awkward people; they upset their friends and make enemies of the Establishment; if their innovation begins to achieve some success, jealousy may move in. Morris fitted this pattern. Although, in rather a naïve way, he expected other local authorities to follow his lead, and looked to the Ministry of Education to back his schemes, he hardly went out of his way tactfully to persuade his colleagues to adopt his ideas. A few did. When this happened he was delighted. But during his lifetime they remained a small minority.

If the majority of his colleagues remained deaf, his message was heard and enthusiastically received by many young people who came under his spell. (A remarkable number of people use this phrase in connection with him.) Often when they first made contact with him they were undergraduates, or teachers, or administrators in Cambridgeshire. And today the natural process of retirement, death and promotion has brought these people into positions of power in government, in education offices and in schools. From such points of vantage they are promoting Morris's ideas which they had heard directly from him when they were (to use William James's phrase) 'in the plastic state'.

The first village college to be founded outside Cambridgeshire was in the neighbouring Soke of Peterborough, where Leslie Tait was chief education officer. This was the Arthur Mellows Village College at Glinton. The first head, P. H. J. Harvey, came from the Linton Village College. Morris was a guest at the opening by the Minister of Education, George Tomlinson, in 1949. Morris himself performed the opening ceremony at the Hope Valley Village College in Derbyshire in 1958. The chief education officer was Jack Longland (now Sir Jack Longland). He has confirmed that Hope Valley was definitely based on Henry Morris's village colleges. His first introduction to the idea was during an official visit to Cambridgeshire with his chairman when he was chief officer in Dorset (1942–49). Derbyshire now has a number of community schools which incorporate, in one way or another, the pattern established in Cambridgeshire.

Devonshire is another county where the tradition of community schools is now firmly established. It reaches back to the early connection between Henry Morris and Elmslie Philip, who was chief education officer from 1941 to 1967. He first met Morris when an undergraduate at King's (1925–28). In 1934 he spent a year as an unpaid assistant to Morris in Shire Hall. He became a frequent guest at Trinity Street and later at the Granary.

When Elmslie Philip presented his proposals for the county development plan to the Devon Education Committee in 1945 he did not disguise the source of his suggestions:

Not only from the economic point of view, but for other cogent social and educational reasons, there is a great deal to be said for the planning of secondary schools, county colleges and adult community centres as cultural units on the lines of the Village Colleges of Cambridgeshire; It is often said that adults (and young people too) do not like to 'go back to school'. This is an unreal attitude. The answer is that in years to come we shall find ourselves thinking more in terms of social, educational and recreational centres, whether in towns or villages, of which one part is devoted to the education of children during some of the daytime.

Devon people may at first move slowly, for it was twenty years before the idea came up there again. But today there are nine community colleges in Devon, and more are envisaged. The first was opened in 1967 at Ilfracombe. The first warden, J. F. Gale, came from being warden of the village college at Swavesey. He was also the first chairman of the county working party on the development of community colleges in the county. This committee's second report, which appeared in 1970, forms the basis of Devon's plans for developing community colleges. But Gale's involvement with community education reaches further back than Swavesey to the time he was working as an adult tutor in Leicestershire under Stewart Mason, the chief education officer.

Stewart Mason's generous acknowledgement of his debt to Morris in the matter of art in schools has already been mentioned (p. 92). He has been equally open about the Cambridgeshire connection with community colleges for which he has been responsible in Leicestershire. In the memorandum on community education which he presented to his committee in 1949 he referred to community schools being 'pioneered by the Cambridgeshire village colleges'. He explained that it was only possible to provide facilities in the countryside equal to those of the towns by linking up the secondary school with adult activities 'along the lines of the Cambridge village college experiment'.

In the same memorandum he echoed Morris in developing the point that the village college idea need not be confined to a rural setting, and also, like Morris and others, pointed out that those who opposed the experiment because people 'would not want to go back to school' were totally mistaken; they did not realise that the school which they would go back to would no longer have the juvenile atmosphere of traditional schools.

Mason rejected the name 'village college', 'which would scarcely be appropriate for Leicestershire' where they would be found in urban as well as rural areas. But he followed Morris in adopting the name, and much more important the function of Warden for the college, 'who will combine in one office the duties of headmaster and warden of the community centre'.

Others have noted the connection between Leicestershire and Cambridgeshire. Bernard Harvey, adviser for Further Education in Leicestershire, states in an article in *Studies in Adult Education* (*Vol 3, No 2*):

The Village College, Morris said, should be seen not as a secondary school with special facilities for further education, but as a community centre housed in a secondary school. His ideal was that 'there should be a grouping and co-ordination of all educational and social agencies . . . an amalgamation which will assemble them into a whole'. It is this concept of a new educational institution which is emerging in Leicestershire.

The Leicestershire-Cambridgeshire link is also noted by Cyril Poster. Of one of the latest Leicestershire Community Colleges [37], he writes: 'The antecedents of Countesthorpe are clearly identifiable in the Cambridgeshire Village Colleges.' The present head of Countesthorpe is John Watts, who started his career at Sawston and went later to open a community school at Les Quennevais, in Jersey (p. 43).

In 1949 Stewart Mason drew up his Leicestershire plan for community education, and in 1954 the first community college in Leicestershire was established at Ashby de la Zouche. The head, Stanley Western, came from Bottisham Village College.

In the neighbouring county of Nottinghamshire, the community school idea has been realised as much by the county architect, Henry Swain, as by the education department. They work closely together. Before being appointed to Nottinghamshire, Swain worked in Hertfordshire with Stirrat Johnson Marshall. Swain acknowledges his debt to Henry Morris with generous enthusiasm:

It fascinates me that he spoke at the RIBA in 1956 on community schools. And no one really heard what he was saying. And now suddenly, for a variety of reasons here it all starts up as if he were alive. It is not just in school design that his work is important, but really in the construction of our towns and cities. The concept of the community school at last makes sense of town planning. But our achievements in the building of community comprehensive schools falls short of what they really should be ... that is why I have been at pains to emphasise the work of Henry Morris, because if we do not keep the philosophy of centring our communities on their cultural and leisure activities we are likely to end up with rather pragmatic solutions.

Swain's department has been responsible for designing a number of community schools in Nottinghamshire. The first was at Bingham, where a magnificent theatre and sports hall are used by the school and the community: there is also a bar, where, as Swain points out, 'it is not surprising to see drinking at the same time, members of the school staff, sportsmen in track suits, actors in their make up and leather jacketed motor cyclists'.

The most ambitious and all embracing scheme conceived in Nottinghamshire is the community school at Sutton in Ashfield. It is a community complex in the middle of the town. The design for it emerged only after officials from the County Education, Architects and Planning Departments sounded opinion in Sutton to find out the wishes of the population. As a result this 'school', apart from classrooms, laboratories, staff rooms and library, will include commonrooms, and lecture theatres, a health clinic, a crèche, a day centre for old age pensioners and for physically handicapped adults. The offices of the Youth Employment and of the Probation Service will be there, alongside places to eat and drink and talk, shops, an ice rink, and a theatre.

The local newspapers, announcing the acceptance of the scheme by the council, recall the day in 1925 when the scheme for Sawston was being considered by the Cambridgeshire County Council.

The *Notts Free Press* of 26 February 1971 wrote:

SCHOOL AND CULTURE SCHEME ACCEPTED:
PUTTING SUTTON ON THE MAP

Sutton is to get a million plus re-development of the High Pavement area in a new school cum civic cum social complex. Mr A. R. Davies, Chairman of the Notts County Council asked members to consider not if they could afford it, but if they could afford to turn it down.

J. A. Stone, Deputy Education Officer,[1] echoed the visionary language Morris had used forty-five years before:

Education is not only for children, and in the High Pavement scheme it will be possible for adults and children to study together, to share the coffee bars, the dining rooms, the study areas and the workshops. We are planning a new world and this scheme will be suitable for this new world. The school will be, as it ought to be, a central and essential part of community living in the town.

In Somerset a scheme for twenty-one village colleges was put forward in 1948. Here W. J. Deacon, a friend of Henry Morris since he was an undergraduate at Cambridge in the twenties, was chief education officer from 1937 to 1967. Deacon used the opportunity offered by the 1944 Education Act to incorporate the village college idea with the county college idea. Deacon has pointed out that one of the reasons why the county college was indefinitely delayed was because it was envisaged by the Ministry of Education as a separate institution, parallel to the schools and to the technical colleges. Deacon proposed for Somerset an integrated service based on community or village colleges, which would have been cheaper and educationally more desirable.

Although the county colleges failed to appear, Somerset secondary schools often have Centres for Further and Adult Education attached to them, which contain a lecture room, a common room and a kitchen serving food and drinks to the common room. Deacon maintains that 'this opportunity for mixing food with learning was a device to which Henry attached much importance. He was right, since it had the effect of bringing the students from the many different types of classes together for conversation in the intervals between classes, creating valuable episodes of "a popular university".' Deacon also insisted that the head of the secondary school should have control also over the adult centre, the same policy as Leicestershire and of course, Cambridgeshire. The Morris connection in Somerset is still maintained through a member of the Education Committee, Ian Phillips, whose name has appeared several times in this book as a loyal friend and generous supporter of Morris and his schemes.

---

1 Later chief education officer of Nottinghamshire.

Assistant to Deacon in Somerset from 1945 to 1949 was Gordon Bessey, who went there from Surrey and later became Chief Education Officer of Cumberland. While in Surrey he had been struck by the disastrous friction which 'dual use' could generate between the school and the further education system under two separate heads. He was therefore attracted to the idea of unitary control inherent in the Cambridgeshire system. In Somerset he continued to develop a lifelong interest in the idea of the community school, got to know Henry Morris, and worked directly on the Somerset Plan of 1948. He writes of Morris in a letter (April 1971): 'His is a name I use frequently in Cumberland, and indeed we, in common with other education authorities, are today interpreting and developing his vision in our community schools.'

Cumberland has developed a number of community schools, probably the best known of these being Wyndham School at Egremont, which was described by Anne Corbett in *New Society* of 27 February 1969:

You can learn something about Wyndham School as you walk down the town main street. The school is there right in the centre. No gates, no high walls. Instead a broad path which draws you into the school and through it. It symbolises better than any badge or motto what the school stands for, a school for the community, accessible, useful.

Morris was always at pains to point out, especially after he joined the New Towns Commission, that the idea of the village college was transferable to cities. The Cheetham-Crumpsall project in Manchester offers the most ambitious example, though Coventry has been the first large city to establish community schools in the inner city area. Here the chief education officer is Robert Aitken, who started his career under Leslie Tait in Peterborough, when the Arthur Mellows College was being planned in the late forties. Aitken has written that he hopes that the newest community school in Coventry, the Sidney Stringer School, set in a densely populated area containing many immigrant families, will have the ethos of a working men's club.

The schools and local authorities so far mentioned by no means exhaust the list of those which have been directly or indirectly related to the ideas of Henry Morris and the village colleges of Cambridgeshire. A valuable account of the community schools as they are today is provided in Cyril Poster's *School and the Community* [37]. Poster in fact is head of a community school on the Isle of Sheppey; he ran the Lawrence Weston Comprehensive School at Bristol as a community centre; and he had previously taught at Bottisham Village College. He too in his book is a strong advocate of unitary control, and scornful of schools where there is 'a Kiplingesque division between day and evening activities'.

In Cheshire an interesting new development is taking place, the establishment of a centre for the community, based on a primary school. At Tattenhall, the Park County Primary School is not only an attractive, unfenced open-plan primary school, it is designed as a meeting place for parents and other adults. The village room, the country branch library and a coffee bar form a part of the building but with the school hall and a separate audio-visual room they can be isolated from the school and used for meetings and discussions. A small swimming bath has been built by the Parents' Association with a grant from the Local Authority. An extensive general recreation area has been provided by the Rural District Council; and a village green by the Parish Council, coextensive with the school playing fields. In Runcorn New Town, also part of the Cheshire authority, two similar projects are being realised. Other community primary schools are at the planning stage for other parts of the county. These new developments are being watched over with special interest by one of the Cheshire education officers, P. J. Field, who served in Cambridgeshire under Henry Morris between 1949 and 1955 and who has written of the Tattenhall project: 'It can trace its ancestry certainly in part to the village college concept. In this instance we are doing something to strengthen the villages; and this perhaps counteracts a tendency which "anti-village collegers" often protested about.'

The idea of the community primary school is not confined to Cheshire; in Cambridgeshire the same idea is being developed. There are already six primary schools which make special arrangements for community activities, originating in the village to take place in the school; the head receives an addition to his salary in recognition of his increased responsibilities, and a member of staff, the community teacher, is appointed, one-third of whose time is allocated to adult and youth activities in the school. The managers include representatives of the adult users of the premises.

So the demonstration area of Cambridgeshire, recommended by Morris in his *Memorandum* of 1924, continues to put up new shoots, while on the national scene the Department of Education and Science, so often opposed to Morris and his ideas, issues circulars to local authorities encouraging them to plan their new schools 'with community use in mind' (Circular 2/70).

But the village college idea, in the mind of Henry Morris, was much bigger than buildings. Through this idea he pointed the way to lifelong education – *'education will be co-terminous with life'* or more picturesquely: *'we will lift the school leaving age to 90'*. He pointed the way to the Deschooled Society: *'We must do away with the insulated school'*. *'Every local community must become an educational society'*. He foresaw the need for localised community control: *'The Village College will become the training ground for a rural democracy realising its social and political duties. The whole welfare of communities and the vigour and prosperity of their intellectual and social life depend on the extent to which initiative can be developed within them.'*

So Morris's influence, through the continuing success of Digswell, and of the village colleges, through the developing community school in town and countryside, lives on. It is the influence of a great and extraordinary educator. For while he enriched the lives of those of us who knew him, he has opened up opportunities for good living and good learning to millions who will never know even his name.

But perhaps his greatest contribution to the 1970s and beyond lies in two lessons which he ceaselessly taught, and which seemingly we still need to learn. First he insisted in the need for all administrators, executives, decision takers, to base their action, not on efficiency (this, as he said, is attained by ants and bees), but on a philosophy which reminds them constantly what life here is for. Secondly he showed, and I hope that this book has gone some way to show, that the most maverick individual can work within the system, can bend it to constructive ends, and can yet retain humanity, integrity, and sensitivity.

THE VILLAGE COLLEGE

Being a Memorandum on the Provision of Educational and Social Facilities for the Countryside, with Special Reference to Cambridgeshire

BY

H. MORRIS

Secretary for Education,
Cambridgeshire

CAMBRIDGE

Printed at the University Press

1925

Facsimile of second edition of the *Memorandum*.

'The rural problem is one that successive governments have ignored in despair. The elementary School buildings are inadequate and insanitary in an appalling proportion of cases; the lack of facilities for continued and secondary education is a disgrace to a highly organised community. All [the necessary] things can be done. What we wish to emphasise is the fact that in rural districts they are not being done, and do not seem likely to be done.'

The Times Educational Supplement
Dec. 13, 1924

EDUCATION AND RURAL WELFARE

I. The immense development of the State system of education in England during the nineteenth and present centuries has been almost wholly an urban development. The towns are rich, and as they are centres of large populations the provision of schools and institutes for higher education has not been administratively difficult because the pupils live in hundreds and thousands at their very doors. The elementary schools of the towns are, on the whole, better built and more generously staffed and equipped than those of the countryside; secondary schools, with a few exceptions, are situated in the towns; so also are the centres of technical education. The most vigorous and systematic popular movement for adult education, the Workers' Educational Association, is an urban movement with comparatively little influence in the villages; there is no corresponding movement for advanced higher education in the countryside.

There are two obvious reasons for the less vigorous development of education in the countryside – its inferior economic position, as compared with the urban centres of industry, and the size and scattered character of the villages which do not lend themselves to easy organisation for the purposes of education and recreational life.

II. Educationally the countryside is subordinate to the towns and its schools are dominated by, and are subservient to, the urban system of secondary and higher education. Owing to the operation of the free-place scholarships system, the abler children are taken from the country schools into the town secondary schools, where they receive a predominantly literary and academic education under urban conditions divorced from the life and habits of the countryside. Either they are lost to the villages and become town workers, or return to their homes unfitted and untrained for life as countrymen and countrywomen. If, as seems possible, the number of urban secondary schools is increased, and the proportion of free places is universally raised from 25 to 40 per cent, the plight of the countryside will be intensified. Already many Education Authorities, confronted with the demand for increased secondary education, are considering schemes for additional secondary and central schools in the town to which country children are to be conveyed on a large scale by train and fleets of motor omnibuses.

With the realisation that the welfare of the countryside depends on 'better farming and better living', much is now being done by the State and by voluntary effort. But adult agricultural education, whether itinerant or centralised in residential colleges and farm institutes, the Women's Institute movement, Rural Libraries, Village Halls, Rural Community Councils, admirable as they are, are nor radical and comprehensive enough to bring about the reconstruction of the countryside.

III. The need of the countryside will not be met until, by a recasting of the rural elementary school system, the villages are provided with an education primary and secondary, which will fit boys and girls for life (in its widest sense) as countrymen and countrywomen;[1] until the countryside is provided with an institution in which the wide provisions of the great consolidated Education Act of 1921, especially in regard to higher and technical education, can be applied to and expressed in terms of rural life and industry; until the population of the countryside has guaranteed to it a social and recreational life based on stable foundations. This view is confirmed by that taken in the recently published *Final Report of the Agricultural Tribunal of Investigation*. In his review of the Report in the *Economic Journal* (September, 1924), Mr J. A. Venn, the Gilbey Lecturer in the History and Economics of Agriculture in the University of Cambridge, says:

The importance they (Sir William Ashley and Professor W. G. S. Adams) attach to education, using the word in its widest sense, will be seen when it is stated that, out of the forty-four recommendations contained in this part of the Report, no less than twenty-five are concerned with the means of organising the farmer and of improving his knowledge, not only of the industry itself, but also of its surroundings.

But if we wish to build up a rural civilisation that will have chronic vigour the first essential is that the countryside should have a localised and indigenous system of education in its own right beginning with the child in the primary school. Itinerant adult agricultural education, rural libraries and village halls, will always be fighting a battle already half lost, if leaving the village system of elementary education as it is, we forget the children and the older boys and girls, and allow the ablest of them to be stolen by the secondary schools of the towns.

THE PROBLEM OF THE VILLAGE SCHOOL

IV. The first step towards providing the countryside with a more efficient education will lie in the reorganisation of the village schools into a system of Senior or Central Schools in the larger villages, supported by tributary junior schools for children under the age of eleven in the smaller surrounding villages. The reasons in favour of such a policy are well known and need only be briefly recapitulated.

In Cambridgeshire for example there are 33 schools with an average attendance below 30, 14 schools with an average attendance between 30 and 40, 14 schools with an average attendance between 40 and 50, 12 schools with an average attendance between 50 and 60, and 41 schools with an average attendance between 60 and 100. Only 21 schools have an average attendance of between 100 and 250.

In these small schools all the children from 3 to 14 years of age are either housed in a single room, or if there is a separate classroom for the infants, all the children above standard I occupy the main room. The main room is sometimes divided by a curtain, less often by a screen. Children of varying ages and varying standards of attainment are necessarily grouped in a single class.

1 Such an education will not unfit them for life in any sphere, whether in the country or the town; or prevent those who are fitted from entering upon any form of higher education of an academic type; nor need the training given commit the error of being 'prematurely vocational.'

The older children perhaps suffer most – they mark time after the age of 11 or 12; the staff is not large enough to meet their special needs, and if it were, the equipment and accommodation for more advanced instruction is lacking.

In brief, the village school with an average attendance of 100 and under is not susceptible of organisation on any sound principle and the small numbers do not allow of the provision of the staff, accommodation, and equipment, which make a wider curriculum possible. The small school is both inadequate and expensive.

V. An illustration of what happens when the schools of an area are grouped in accordance with a plan is afforded in the Burwell area of Cambridgeshire. In Burwell there were four schools, three voluntary schools and one Council School, each working as a separate entity. One old Church School was closed: the two other church schools were organised as junior schools for the children under 10, and the Council School as a Senior School for those over 10 years. The Senior School was enlarged by the addition of a room for handicrafts and domestic subjects and land for a school garden was hired. Later, the older children from the neighbouring villages of Reach and Swaffham Prior were transferred to the Burwell Senior School.

At Burwell Senior School there are 150 children of 10–15 years of age. They are graded in classes according to age and attainment, each under the charge of a qualified teacher. Handicrafts, domestic subjects and gardening form an integral part of the training. Great importance is attached to the teaching of English (the school produces a play once a year), to local history and to physical training. There is a strong corporate life and there are thriving athletic and hobby clubs. The school has its colours, with a school cap for the boys, and a smock and cap for the girls. The children travelling from a distance take their midday meal together under the charge of a teacher.

VI. The ultimate aim of the Cambridgeshire scheme is to establish some 30–40 senior or central schools under the charge of graduates or specially qualified head teachers. It is hoped then to concentrate all the older children of the county in these centres, and to give them there advanced instruction with a strong rural bias in schools adequately equipped and staffed. Three important results will follow. The numbers of older children in attendance at the Senior Schools will make possible the organisation of a class system in each school that will have regard to age and attainments. It will be possible to concentrate the facilities for handicrafts, domestic subjects, general elementary science, and gardening in a limited number of centres. At the same time the staffs at the tributary schools, relieved of the responsibility of the older children, will be able to devote themselves effectively to the needs of the infant and junior children.

The Cambridgeshire grouping scheme has had two interesting results:

(a) The Senior Schools have made it possible to attract a new type of teacher to the countryside. Apart from specially qualified teachers, there are now eight head and assistant teachers in Cambridgeshire who are graduates of Oxford, Cambridge, London, Glasgow and Birmingham.

(b) Owing to the difficulties inherent in the dual system of voluntary and Council Schools, the Education Committee set up an advisory Committee representative of all denominations and of the teaching profession and presided over by the Vice-Chancellor of the University (Dr E. C. Pearce, Master of

Corpus Christi College) with the object of arriving at an agreed syllabus of religious teaching. The work of the Committee was successful and resulted in what is known as the 'Cambridgeshire Concordat', which includes the *Cambridgeshire Syllabus of Religious Teaching for Schools*. Two Bibles based on the syllabus ('The Little Children's Bible' and 'The Children's Bible'), edited by Professor Alexander Nairne, Sir Arthur Quiller-Couch, and Dr T. R. Glover have been published and are in use in Cambridgeshire Schools. (The sales of the Children's Bibles in Great Britain have reached 60,000, and an American edition has been published by Messrs Macmillan.)

VII. The grouping of the schools of the countryside on the lines just described will have consequences of profound importance in rural England. In course of time the vast congeries of rural schools will be formed into an ordered system of two types of school, for those under eleven years or thereabouts and those over that age. With the assignment of a defined and comprehensible function to all the schools, there will accrue immense gains in organisation, in the economical provision of buildings and equipment, in the development and enrichment of the curriculum, and in the training of the teachers. Money will be saved and better spent. The system will be such as to allow, as and when circumstances demand, of the easy and natural development of centrally-situated rural secondary schools. There will at last be possible all over the English countryside a rural education of a secondary type for the training of boys and girls for life as countrymen and countrywomen.

THE VILLAGE COLLEGE

VIII. But if rural England is to have the education it needs and the social and recreational life it deserves, more is required than the reorganisation of the elementary school system; and that which is required is possible.

There must be a grouping and co-ordination of all the educational and social agencies which now exist in isolation in the countryside: an amalgamation which, while preserving the individuality and function of each, will assemble them into a whole and make possible their expression for the first time in a new institution, single but many-sided, for the countryside.

IX. What this means may be shown in detail.

The County Council is the Statutory Authority for:

(i) Education:
   Elementary.
   Higher:
   (*a*) Secondary Education and Day Continuation Schools
   (*b*) Further Education.
   (*c*) Agricultural Education.
(ii) The Public Libraries Act, 1919.
(iii) Juvenile Employment and Unemployment Insurance.
(iv) Public Health.
(v) Agriculture (including the lesser rural industries).

The County Council is therefore the Statutory Authority for the whole of the legislation which provides for the social and economic welfare of the countryside by means of educational, recreational and community facilities,[1]

---

1 By community facilities are meant parochial buildings for non-ecclesiastical purposes, recreation grounds, etc., and *not* services provided, *e.g.* by the Rural District Council as the 'Sanitary Authority'.

except that in regard to the two latter, its powers are shared by the Rural District and Parish Councils. But the functions of the major Statutory Authority are carried out in separation in the village, and there is no co-ordination of County Council services with those of the minor local authority. The main reason for this is that the village elementary school is not adequate to the wide conception of education as covering all ages and activities and including social and physical training as it is expressed in the consolidated Education Act of 1921. In most, if not all, villages there will be found, side by side with a piece of elementary education, a group of evening classes held in the elementary school if no other building is available. There may be a Women's Institute Class and a British Legion Class; a Choral Class in a private house; and one or two Agricultural Education Classes held either in the school, or in the parish hall, or in a barn or other farm buildings.[1] The branch of the County Library has no appropriate home – it is housed in a corner of the school or hall or in a private residence.[2] The recreation ground belonging to the Parish Council is stationed in an outlying corner of the village. If there is an Infant Welfare Centre, that is housed in another corner.

The existing activities are not only carried on in isolation from one another, but the greater number are not suitably accommodated. Again, the existing elementary school building does not allow of the development of fuller educational facilities for young people and adults. Finally, if there is no suitable village hall, the Voluntary Associations of the countryside have no place in which to meet except the children's school; there a large number of social gatherings must be held; and there even, accommodation for the work of village local government must by law be found rent free.

X. All the activities and facilities that already exist in the countryside, and all those which by statute could be provided, should be brought together in and around one institution.

In Cambridgeshire the aim would be to establish in about ten carefully selected centres where Senior Schools are already organised, a system of village colleges which would provide for the co-ordination and development of all forms of education – primary, secondary, further and adult education, including agricultural education – together with social and recreational facilities, and at the same time furnish a community centre for the neighbourhood.

In these centres the isolated elementary school as such, with all the narrower conceptions associated with it, would be abolished; it would be absorbed into a larger institution.

Let us, for sake of illustration, visualise the village college as consisting of two wings or three-sided courts, one containing the school portion, the other accommodation for adult activities, and with the village hall between, thus:

1 Everybody with experience of rural adult education knows that one of the greatest handicaps is the lack of an appropriate building, and that young people and adults do not like going back to the elementary school with its juvenile atmosphere and desks and equipment.
2 An almost universal need is felt in the villages for a worthy home for the library, with room for reading during the long winter evenings when the small cottage is filled by the family and the light is none too good for reading.

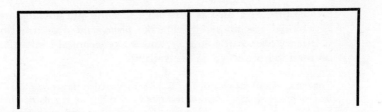

The village college would provide for the following:

(1) A nursery schoolroom which would also serve for use as an Infant Welfare Centre.

(2) A primary school for the children of 5–10 years of age of the central village only.

(3) A school providing a rural education of a secondary type for children from 10–15 or 16 years in the central village and the tributary villages of the chosen area. Such tributary villages would be within reasonable walking or cycling or train or motor-omnibus distance (on the average 2–3½ miles in Cambridgeshire); and the tributary villages would retain a junior school for infants and juniors up to the age of 10 years. The school thus forming part of the village college would in addition to classrooms contain a workshop for handicrafts, a room for domestic science (cookery, laundry, house-wifery, etc.) and a room for general elementary science. These three rooms would also be used for evening adult education in crafts, domestic subjects and agricultural science.

(4) A staff room for teachers, and the usual offices for teachers and children.

(5) The village hall, which would serve
    (*a*) for use in the day, as a school assembly hall, for the midday meal, school functions, physical training and school plays and concerts;
    (*b*) in the evenings, for broadcast programmes at stated hours, concerts, performances by the village dramatic society, exhibitions by the travelling cinema of the Cambridgeshire Rural Community Council, lectures, dances, whist drives and public meetings.

(6) A room divided into two parts – a library section containing a permanent nucleus of books and the monthly supply of books from the Cambridge-shire County Library, where villagers could read and study in peace and reasonable comfort; and a reading-room section containing newspapers and periodicals.

The Library would thus be intimately associated with every stage and type of educational work carried on in the college, and would be used by every student from the youngest to the oldest. A new conception of the Public Library as that department which provides the educational tool known as 'books' would be realised. Schoolboys and girls, their older sisters and brothers, and their parents would freely pass to and fro between classroom or lecture-room or the demonstration plot and the Library.

(7) A room definitely set apart for agricultural education, containing maps, charts and specimens, to be used jointly with the science laboratory (Paragraph (3)).

Such a room with the laboratory would provide for the theoretical portion of that type of agricultural education – Local Courses and Local Instruction – which in accordance with the scheme of the Ministry of Agriculture does not come within the scope of the Farm Institute. The village college would also be the natural centre near which instruction in manual processes such as thatching, hedging and ditching and the use of agricultural machinery, would take place, and demonstrations given in veterinary science and farriery; and where technical instruction and advice on rural industries would be available.

The demonstrations of crops would be organised at farms near the village college. In Cambridgeshire all demonstrations carried out by the Agricultural Education Sub-Committee of the Education Committee would thus be concentrated in village college centres, and could be co-ordinated with the work of the school and also with the adult Agricultural Courses given in the college. The village college would then form a centre for agricultural and horticultural education.

(8) Two or three rooms primarily for adult evening classes, and also for village meetings connected with the Women's Institutes, the British Legion, Boy Scouts and Girl Guides, and committee meetings connected with village activities such as the Horticultural and Flower Show, the Summer Festival and Athletic Sports, the Village Football, Cricket and Tennis Clubs, and for such activities of rural local government as must by law be accommodated in a public elementary school if no other public building is available, *e.g.* Parish Council meetings, local government inquiries, meetings under the Allotment Acts, Candidature for persons for either district or parish councils, any parish or local government committees appointed to administer public funds and endowments within the parish (Local Government Act 1824, Sect. 4).

(9) Simple shower baths and a dressing room (both in a basement) for the use the school children, and of the Athletic Clubs of the village. (Village athletes hardly ever enjoy the luxury of a hot bath and rub-down after the game!)

(10) The village recreation grounds provided by the Parish Council alongside. This would provide additional playing-field accommodation without extra cost for all the children at the school, and would take the place of the old asphalt or concrete schoolyard.

(11) A plot of ground to serve for a school garden, and for the smaller demonstrations in horticulture.

(12) A centre for carrying out the Education Authority's work connected with Choice of Employment and Juvenile Unemployment Insurance.

(13) The Warden's House.

(14) Accommodation for Indoor Recreations. There is nothing to prevent the Local Education Authority renting the rooms of a County Council building for recreational purposes, such as clubs and games. And it should not be forgotten that the Local Education Authority have powers under Section 86 of the Education Act, 1921, to provide facilities for social and physical training for children, young persons, and adults. But a centre such as that in which the village college is situated might reasonably and naturally require accommodation explicitly set apart for indoor games, especially billiards, and controlled by village trustees.

It is important and essential that the accommodation for such indoor recreations should not be disassociated from the village college, if that institution is to realise its functions as a community centre for the area – educational and social.

The following is put forward as a perfectly satisfactory solution of this problem:

(*a*) As in the case of many Central and Secondary Schools the school buildings or other part of the village college could be utilised in the evenings for boys' and girls' clubs, the Debating Society, the Chess Club, the Dramatic Club, the Natural History Club, the Photography Club, and indoor games.

(*b*) The block containing a billiard room and one or more small rooms for the various indoor games could be built adjacent to the college. The two buildings need only be separated by a few yards; they would be actively associated in use in daily life and habit, though administratively they would be separate entities.

Such recreation rooms would be provided out of voluntary funds; or if thus associated with a village college they might be made eligible for a grant from any funds set aside for the purpose by the Development Commissioners and the Ministry of Agriculture. They would be under proper control, *i.e.* of trustees consisting of the Village Social Council.

(*c*) *On the other hand, there is nothing to prevent the recreation room expressly forming a part of the village college; and it would be interesting if the Development Commissioners and the Ministry of Agriculture, co-operating with the Board of Education and the Local Education Authority (regard being had to the latter's powers under Section 86 of the Education Act, 1921) followed out this plan for experimental purposes if a village college is established in Cambridgeshire.*

It should be noted that a building serving all the needs enumerated in Paragraphs (1) – (14) can be provided and maintained by the Statutory Authority.

All that part concerning elementary and higher education (including school garden and playground) would rank for grant from the Board of Education. All the services of elementary and higher education carried on within its walls would be statutory service provided and maintained by the Local Authority and aided by the Board of Education.

The services of agricultural education would be eligible for the 66⅔ per cent maintenance grants of the Ministry of Agriculture who also have power to contribute a grant of 75 per cent towards the capital cost of any part of the building not eligible for grant from the Board of Education and used primarily for agricultural education for persons over the age of 16 years.

The capital cost and the maintenance of the Library and Reading-room section of the building would be a rate aided service only, except in so far as it might be possible for the Board of Education and the Ministry of Agriculture to contribute to the capital cost and maintenance on account of work done in connection with elementary and higher and agricultural education. (*See* Paragraph (6) above.)

The hall portion would be eligible for the grant of the Board of Education as it would be an integral part of the school and would be available for social and physical training under Section 86 of the Education Act of 1921.

In this connection the assistance of the Ministry of Agriculture and the Development Commissioners who are considering the question of grants to village halls might be enlisted.

It may be noted that in all villages the premises of council schools which are the property of the Local Authority are rented for general purposes and when not required for educational purposes; and this would apply to village colleges.

The recreation ground is a service provided by the Parish Council;

associated with it might be any land provided by the Education Authority as a playing-field under Section 86 of the Education Act of 1921.

XI. *Government.* The control of the village college would be vested in a body of governors responsible to the Local Authority, consisting of

(*a*) The managers of the elementary school. As the school would serve more than one village, such a body would by statute be a composite body consisting of managers appointed by the County Council, and managers appointed by the minor local authorities of the area served.

(*b*) Members appointed by the County Council as representing local interests, to supervise higher, including agricultural, education.

The Parish Councils (or Parish Meetings) as statutory minor local authorities for elementary education might appropriately be associated with the supervision of higher education.

(*c*) A representative appointed by the Senate of the University of Cambridge.

(*d*) Representatives of other interests, *e.g.* the Parish Council as owners of the recreation ground.

The body of governors would be appointed under an approved scheme providing for the proper discharge of statutory functions. The body of governors when acting as a *whole* would act in an advisory and consultative capacity only except when they might as a whole properly act executively, as for example, in regard to all forms of higher education. Executive acts in regard to certain other services would devolve on the constituent section statutorily responsible, as for example, in the case of the elementary school on the managers. The governing body in so far as it carried out services for which the County Council is the Local Authority would be responsible to the County Council.

XII. *Head of the Village College.* The Head of the village college following on the coordination of educational services, would combine several functions. A new type of leader and teacher with a higher status and of superior calibre would at last be possible in the English countryside. An appropriate title expressing this new status and wider scope is therefore required – especially if we are to escape from the old conception of the Village Schoolmaster. He might be styled the *Warden* – we should read then of the *Warden of Sawston*; the *Warden of Bourn*; and why not *Provost*, or *Master*, or *Principal* in some cases?

He would have to be a man country-bred and trained at a University; a Science Degree would be an additional qualification; above all he would have to be a man with a love of and understanding of rural life, with powers of leadership.

As Headmaster of the school he would be entitled to the appropriate salary under the allocated Standard Scale; in addition he would be paid sums for duties supervisory and otherwise in connection with higher education.

The scope of the Warden's duties, the amount of his remuneration, and the allocation of proportions of it, *e.g.* to Elementary Education (or to Secondary Education if the School within the College is designed to comply with the Regulations for Secondary Schools), Further Education (and perhaps Agricultural Education) are questions that require more detailed treatment than is possible in this brief memorandum. The problem is one that would best be stated not in the abstract, but when specific proposals for a village college are formulated to the Board of Education (and the Ministry of Agriculture).

XIII. *Architecture.* The possibility of bringing together all the various educational and social services that would find a habitation within the village college, the possibility of achieving this remarkable synthesis depends in the first place on the provision of the building.

The building that will form the village college will be so new in English architecture, and its significance so great, that the design and construction of the first village colleges should be very carefully provided for. For we are in measurable sight, if we use imagination and have adminstrative courage, of giving to the English countryside a number of fine and worthy public buildings. The schools of rural England are nearly always bad and seldom beautiful – never a form of art, as they might and ought to be. The greater portion of them were designed to serve the joint purpose of a school and parish hall, and at a time when the standard of staffing and accommodation, the quality of the curriculum and the conception of teaching were vastly inferior to those of our own day. As the Education Act of 1921 is progressively put into operation, the buildings are bound to be replaced. During the next few decades large numbers of new educational buildings costing large sums of money will spring up in England and Wales, and the process will be accelerated if, as seems possible, the system of 'dual control' of Voluntary and Council Schools is abolished within the lifetime of the present Government. There is no reason why the erection of the new buildings should not be made the opportunity of adding to the public architecture of the countryside; and there is additional reason that the opportunity should not be missed because there is not likely ever to be any other constructive movement so national and widespread, so completely affecting the lives of the whole community, as that of public education. The provision of buildings for the system of public education will in the present century be one of the chiefest ways in which the art of architecture can influence the body politic. If the opportunity is not taken it will only be through dullness and lack of vision.

The difference between good and bad architecture is more often the difference between a good design and a bad design, rather than the difference between cheap and costly material. Assuming that good material will be available for a village college, the important thing is to see that it has a significant design. Such a design must be simple, but it could be beautiful. Using our imagination, let us say to the architect: 'Education is one of our greatest public services and one of the most widely diffused. Every year we spend on it some 80 millions. Every town and every village must have its educational buildings. Education touches every citizen. We have a conception of a new institution for the countryside, an institution that will touch every side of the life of the inhabitants of the district in which it is placed. Will you think out a design for such a building, a village college? A building that will express the spirit of the English countryside which it is intended to grace, something of its humaneness and modesty, something of the age-long and permanent dignity of husbandry; a building that will give the countryside a centre of reference arousing the affection and loyalty of the country child and country people, and conferring significance on their way of life? If this can be done simply and effectually, and the varying needs which the village college will serve realised as an entity and epitomised in a building, a standard may be set and a great tradition may be begun; in such a synthesis architecture will find a fresh and widespread means of expression. If the village college is a true and workable conception, the institution will, with various modifications, speed over rural England; and in course of time a new series of worthy public buildings will stand side by side with the parish churches of the countryside.'

XIV. The village college as thus outlined would not create something superfluous; it would not be a spectacular experiment and a costly luxury. It would take all the various vital but isolated activities in village life – the School, the Village Hall and Reading Room, the Evening Classes, the Agricultural Education Courses, the Women's Institute, the British Legion, Boy Scouts and Girl Guides, the recreation ground, the branch of the County Rural Library, the Athletic and Recreation Clubs – and, bringing them together into relation, create a new institution for the English countryside. It would create out of discrete elements an organic whole; the vitality of the constituent elements would be preserved, and not destroyed, but the unity they would form would be a new thing. For, as in the case of all organic unities, the whole is greater than the mere sum of the parts. It would be a true social synthesis – it would take existing and live elements and bring them into a new and unique relationship.

§ The village college would change the whole face of the problem of rural education. As the community centre of the neighbourhood it would provide for the whole man, and abolish the duality of education and ordinary life. It would not only be the training ground for the art of living, but the place in which life is lived, the environment of a genuine corporate life. The dismal dispute of vocational and non-vocational education would not arise in it. It would be a visible demonstration in stone of the continuity and never ceasingness of education. There would be no 'leaving school'! – the child would enter at three and leave the college only in extreme old age.[1] It would have the great virtue of being local so that it would enhance the quality of actual life as it is lived from day to day – the supreme object of education. Unlike non-local residential institutions (the public schools, the universities, the few residential workingmen's colleges, and, to take a continental example, the Danish High Schools) it would not be divorced from the normal environment of those who would frequent it from day to day, or from that greater educational institution, the family. Has there ever been an educational institution that at one and the same time provided for the needs of the whole family and consolidated its life – its social, physical, intellectual and economic life? Our modern educational institutions provide only for units of the family, or separate the individual from the family by time and space so that they may educate it apart and under less natural conditions. The village college would lie athwart the daily lives of the community it served; and in it the conditions would be realised under which education would be not an escape from reality, but an enrichment and transformation of it. For education is committed to the view that the ideal order and the actual order can ultimately be made one.

§ We are witnessing in this country through the extension of the principle of ownership the disappearance of the old land owning class, and at the same time a modification of the influence and authority of the Squire and the Parson. There are social and political, as well as economic problems, arising out of this change. The responsibilities of leadership and the

---

1 In all seriousness it might be said that the 'school leaving age' would be lifted to 90.

maintenance of liberal and humane traditions in our squireless villages (which are the rule not the exception in Cambridgeshire) will fall on a larger number of shoulders – they will fall on the whole community. The village college will be the seat and guardian of humane public traditions in the countryside, the training ground of a rural democracy realising its social and political duties. Without some such institution as the village college a rural community consisting largely of agricultural workers, small proprietors and small farmers will not be equal to the task of maintaining a worthy rural civilisation. The alternative would be a countryside like that in some continental countries, prosperous perhaps, but narrow and material-istic, without native distinction and charm, and with no instinct for even the popular arts.

§ The village college by linking up the local representatives of the county authority with the minor local authorities and uniting them in the concrete task of administering a many-sided local institution and powers visibly affecting the life around them from day to day, would revitalise rural local government. The Parish Council, still exercising its own powers, but con-cerned in the exercise of larger ones, would be endowed with new life. Good government and self government might at last be combined in the countryside. Rural local government languishes because there is no insti-tution that provides a centre of reference and a means of expression. The village college would meet that need.

§ The village college would provide the chance for creating for the country-side a new type of village leader and teacher with a new status and a wide function embracing human welfare in its biggest sense – spiritual, physical, social and economic.

§ The village college would provide an opportunity for creative architecture. Our State system of education has not yet produced noble architecture on the same scale as that of all the other great movements of the national spirit. And there has been no public architecture in the English countryside since the Parish Churches were built – that is, since the Middle Ages. Apart from these inheritances from a past age, the biggest and most impressive public buildings in the countryside are the asylums and the workhouses: big asylums and poor schools – a sight to put all Heaven in a rage.

§ The village college would have in it all the conditions of permanence. It will be formed by welding together existing institutions already planted deep in the habits and affections of the people. Its activities will have statutory authority, and statutory financial support, and its financial stability is therefore guaranteed.

§ Finally, the village college would not outlive its function, for the main reason that it would not be committed irrevocably to any intellectual or social dogma or to any sectional point of view. Intellectually it might be one of the freest of our English Institutions.

THE SUGGESTED PLAN FOR CAMBRIDGESHIRE

XV. The County of Cambridge has already been mapped out in a series of about 30–40 areas which should be served by Senior Schools; and on an examination of the areas it appears that there are ten centres at which village colleges could be effectively organised. These centres are:

Sawston	Burwell
Bourn	Cottenham

Harston	Waterbeach
Linton	Weston Colville
Melbourn	Steeple Morden

These centres have been provisionally chosen because they dominate a suitable large and homogeneous area.

An immediate opportunity of establishing two village colleges on an experimental basis has now arisen at Sawston and Bourn. Each of the areas surrounding these two villages presents different features, and would require secondary modifications of the general plan of the village college to fit in with local conditions.

SAWSTON. The population of Sawston is 1530. In addition to agriculture there is an important rural industry – the heating of pelts, which are converted into chamois leather for domestic use and for gloves. There is also a mill employing about 400, engaged in making special kinds of parchment and hand-made papers, for which the waters of the River Granta are used. The neighbouring villages are Whittlesford (population 980), Babraham (population 238), Pampisford (population 255) and Duxford (population 734). These villages are predominantly agricultural, except Whittlesford, which contributes workers to a paper mill and to a works for making agricultural implements.

The school at Sawston is a Council School with an average attendance of 227 and already serves the purpose of a Senior School for a portion of the district.

It occupies a commodious site which could, if necessary, be sold and the proceeds devoted to the purchase of a large site abutting on the recreation ground. The village has no hall at present, though some funds have been collected. A village college at Sawston would be able to provide effectively for the needs of the rural community of an area of five square miles and including typically agricultural villages such as Babraham, Pampisford and Duxford. Such an institution would provide for:

(1) A nursery, infants', and junior school for Sawston only.
(2) A rural school for the children of 10 years to 15 years of Sawston, Whittlesford, Babraham, Pampisford and Duxford.
(3) A community centre for Sawston.
(4) A centre of further adult and agricultural education for the area of Sawston, Whittlesford, Babraham, Pampisford and Duxford.

BOURN. Bourn (population 623) lies at the centre of a tract of purely agricultural country containing the villages of Caxton (population 398), Longstowe (population 249), Kingston (population 173), Caldecote (population 161) and Toft (population 205).

A village college at Bourn would follow the general lines of the college at Sawston. The area is very poorly served both with educational and social facilities, and there would be an opportunity of showing the maximum effect that a composite institution like the village college would have on the educational, social and economic life of a population wholly engaged in agricultural pursuits. At Bourn it would be possible to make the village college the centre of agricultural education and demonstration for young men and women and adults in the surrounding area.

CONCLUSION: CAMBRIDGESHIRE AS A DEMONSTRATION AREA FOR
RURAL RECONSTRUCTION

XVI. The steps by which two experimental examples of a village college could be established in Sawston and Bourn have now been described. But the compact rural County of Cambridgeshire affords a tract of England in which a system of village colleges might be established. Here is Cambridgeshire wholly agricultural with its representative agricultural community; the University in the middle with the great Department of Agricultural and Horticultural Research, and the National Institute of Agricultural Botany; its scheme for grouping rural schools and fashioning an efficient system of rural education; a County system of agricultural and horticultural education; a scheme of rural adult education in working order; a progressive policy of public health; its County Rural Library with a branch in every village; its Rural Community Council working with the assistance of the experts of various Departments of the University; its Council of Musical Education and Musical Festival.

Picture it with its educational, economic and social life reborn by a system of village colleges, starting with Sawston and Bourn, and gradually increased to about ten. If the Carnegie Trustees and the Development Commissioners could father such a scheme, they might perform a work of reconstruction of first-rate national importance. The possibilities are so great that they do not require stressing. The Trustees might initiate an educational advance which would be one of the greatest in the history of state education. They might make possible at last after a generation of discussion a really massive contribution to the rural problem which it could be said without exaggeration would surpass anything that has been done in any country, more comprehensive for instance than the Danish High School Movement.

One swallow does not make a summer; and a single college at Sawston or at Bourn, though it might mark a turning point, would not afford the palpable and concrete demonstration of rural reconstruction as would a tract of rural England like Cambridgeshire its whole life re-orientated by a system of village colleges.

The time is ripe for a great constructive step forward in the rural problem. The work of re-establishing the life and welfare of the countryside is admitted to be really urgent; it is required in the interests of our national life and health. And as we may not always remain predominantly an industrial country, it is necessary that the problem of the reconstruction of the village should be dealt with in good time. There are certain economic aspects of rural welfare that can only be dealt with by governments; but all the other aspects of rural welfare are such as can be dealt with by education (in its widest sense) and by the rebuilding of the social life of the countryside.

And if this great work cannot be carried out in accordance with some such plan as has been briefly described, in what way is it possible to conceive its ever being done?

BIBLIOGRAPHY

I THE WRITINGS AND SPEECHES OF HENRY MORRIS
Copies of the documents marked with an asterisk are lodged with the Chief
Education Officer, Shire Hall, Cambridge.

[1] *The Cambridgeshire Syllabus of Religious Teaching for Schools* Cambridge
University Press 1923

*[2] *The Village College. Being a Memorandum on the provision of Educational and
Social Facilities for the Countryside* Cambridge University Press 1924. Re-
printed here as Appendix, pp. 142–56

*[3] 'Institutionalism and freedom in Education' *New Ideals Quarterly* ii,
March 1926. This was one of the most closely argued expressions of his
philosophy

*[4] 'A modern philosophy of education' review article *The Nation and
Athenaeum* 25 August 1929

*[5] Rural Civilisation. Paper read to the British Association in Blackpool,
15 September 1936

*[6] 'The Danish High School Myth' *Adult Education* December 1941

*[7] Postwar Policy in Education. Paper for the Association of Directors
and Secretaries of Education, 31 July 1941

*[8] The Post Primary Curriculum. Paper for the Association of Direc-
tors and Secretaries of Education, 30 May 1942

[9] The New Senior School in Britain. Broadcast Talk on North American
Service of the BBC, 14 September 1942

*[10] 'Adult education' in *Education Handbook* Norwich, Jarrold 1943,
Ed. E. W. Woodhead, pp. 87–97. This contains the essence of his thought;
he admits here that he quotes liberally from his *New Ideals Quarterly*
article [3] and from two lectures he gave at the Cambridge Institute of
Education in 1925, which have not survived

[11] The Village College. Broadcast talk on Far Eastern Service BBC,
February 1944

[12] Community Centres and the School in Rural and Urban Areas. Paper
read to British Institute of Adult Education, 22 April 1944

[13] Community Centres. Paper read to the Association of Directors and
Secretaries of Education, January 1946

[14] Buildings for Further Education. Paper read to the RIBA, 26 April
1945

[15] Education and Planning. Paper read at the annual conference of the
Town and Country Planning Association, April 1946

*[16] Liberty and the Individual. Broadcast talk, Home Service BBC,
13 November 1946

*[17] Report on the West African Institute of Industries, Arts and Social Science, Colonial Office, November 1947

[18] Amusement and Education. Paper to the All Souls Group, October 1953

[18A] Education, Community Centres, and other cultural institutions (1948). Paper sent to Managers of the Development Corporations of every New Town

*[19] 'The idea of a village college' broadcast talk, Home Service BBC, printed in *The Listener*, 10 February 1955

*[20] The Contemporary Artist and the Community, June 1955

*[21] Architecture, Humanism and the Local Community. Paper read to the RIBA and published in *RIBA Journal* 15 May 1956

[22] Style Maketh Man. Paper read to the Council of Visual Education, 1957

II OTHER WORKS REFERRED TO IN THE TEXT

*[23] ASSOCIATION OF DIRECTORS AND SECRETARIES OF EDUCATION, *Post War Policy*, HMSO 1942 (the Orange Book)

*[24] BIMROSE, DOROTHY *The Story of Digwell: A Matter Done*. Foreword by Henry Moore. Available from the Maynard Gallery, Welwyn Garden City

[25] CENTRAL ADVISORY COUNCIL FOR EDUCATION *Children and Their Primary Schools* (Plowden Report) HMSO 1967

[26] CONSULTATIVE COMMITTEE ON EDUCATION *The Education of the Adolescent* (Hadow Report) HMSO 1926

[27] EDUCATION, BOARD OF *Handbook for Teachers* HMSO 1937

[28] EDUCATION, MINISTRY OF *Community Centres* 1946

[29] EDUCATION, BOARD OF *Handbook of Suggestions for Teachers* HMSO 1947

[30] ELLIS, HAVELOCK *My Confessional* Bodley Head 1934

[31] FARNELL, D. J. 'Henry Morris: a n architect of education' unpublished thesis, Institute of Education, Cambridge. A very valuable source

[32] FISHER, NORMAN 'Henry Morris' *Education* 29 Oct. 1954

[33] FISHER, NORMAN Henry Morris. Pioneer of education in the countryside. Arthur Mellows Memorial Lecture 1965. Available from Arthur Mellows Trust, Glint, Peterborough

[34] GIEDION, S. *Walter Gropius; work and teamwork* Architectural Press 1954

*[35] HOWE, JACK *New College of Further Education Architectural Brief*

[36] PEVSNER, N. *Cambridgeshire: The Buildings of England No. 10* Penguin 1954

[37] POSTER, C. *The School and the Community* Macmillan 1971

[38] POSTER, C. 'Village colleges today' *New Society* 9 Oct. 1969

[39] RASHDALL, HASTING S. *Universities of Europe in the Middle Ages* Oxford University Press 1936

[40] READ, HERBERT *Annals of Innocence and Experience* Faber 1940

[40A] READ, HERBERT *Education Through Art*, Faber 1958

[41] ROBERTSON, BRIAN Introduction to *British Sculpture and Painting* from the collection of the Leicestershire Education Authority, Whitechapel Gallery, London 1967

[42] SCOTT, GEOFFREY *Architecture of Humanism* Constable 1914

INDEX